PRAISE

In her book, *Getting to Forgiveness*, Susie Levan embodies what it means to be a phoenix rising from the ashes with grace and gratitude. Her story of love, success, extreme loss and ultimately finding love within herself is a beautiful message for anyone who has struggled with their own life's purpose and belonging. It is a compelling reminder of the power of forgiveness and what it means to choose the path that ultimately leads to wisdom.

Lisa Lutoff-Perlo
President & CEO
Celebrity Cruises

Susie Levan writes from the heart and from a vast experience. She lives out the notion that if life knocks you down 7 times, you get up 8. However, in her case, she arises grateful for the lessons from the falls. She has opened her heart and painstakingly put to paper the steps that can help each of us live a life of gratitude and gain valuable skills to cope with whatever comes our way.

Penny S. Shaffer, Ph.D.
Market President, South Florida
Florida Blue

This book is not just a compilation of Susie's life's experiences, but a must read for any self-evolved individual interested in improving the human condition and what we can each do to make our own personal imprint around living a life of purpose. Susie teaches us that a life of fulfillment is truly a life of service to others. Susie is and has been an example of how the modern-day woman balances the demands of family, business and community. Susie is an inspiration to anyone that has encountered a life-altering experience. Susie's book teaches us all that our time here is finite and we must be mindful to leave behind a torch to carry our legacies. *Getting to Forgiveness* is a work of art!

Laura Raybin Miller, Commissioner
South Broward Hospital District dba/
Memorial Healthcare System

Fortitude, grace and spiritual strength—these are the words I use to describe Susie Levan. But how does an ordinary woman become these things? It is true that every woman of power has a story; this is Susie Levan's. This book chronicles Susie's incredible journey through personal tribulations, toxic fears, spiritual inquiry and eventual triumph. These are a woman's steps to power.

Elaine M. Wallace, D.O., MS., MS., MS., MS.
Dean--Dr. Kiran C. Patel College of Osteopathic Medicine

Susie Levan radiates light—both in person and through her words in this book. She is a teacher through and through—constantly sharing her light. We are blessed that she has found the incredible courage to share her journey with us and the precious lessons she has discovered along the way, from the heart shattering lows to the moments of radical amazement. These lessons, they are what have brought wisdom into Susie's life. They make her light shine brighter. Thankfully, she has the incredible ability not just to tell her story, but to share her wisdom, her light, with us in a way that touches our hearts and souls. By sharing her story, Susie gives us gifts—tools that empower us to grow as spiritual beings, in doing so, she adds light to all of our lives.

Andrew Jacobs, Rabbi
Ramat Shalom Synagogue
Founder, ISH

I have known Susie Levan initially through membership in The Strategic Forum, a business organization of CEO's and Corporate Executives more than 13 years ago. I was honored to be a Director on her Board, The Work-Life Balance Institute For Women, that produced her publication, *Balance* magazine and to be on the Levan Ambassador's Board for Nova Southeastern University. Throughout this time, I have seen Susie transform into the spiritual, inspirational, motivational individual that she has become and helped so many others — particularly women grow with her essence of giving and predisposition for gratitude. Her book personifies all the life experiences that make her into the woman she is today. With the knowledge and skills she has gained, *Getting to Forgiveness* will empower others to find freedom, fulfilment and release for themselves —to be fearless in finding their soul's purpose on earth. This is a must read.

Sue Romanos, CPC, CTS, CSP
CEO, Emeritus
CAREERXCHANGE®, Inc.

Susie's NDE (Near-Death Experience) is so magical that I read it twice, so that I'd never forget it.

Life can be long, sometimes monotonous. It can be easy to question if there is an overall plan, or anyone watching over us. Susie's spiritual memoir, *Getting to Forgiveness*, is a life-affirming story of magic and mystery, told with great wisdom.

Linda Sivertsen
Bestselling Author, Host of Beautiful Writers Podcast

Levan is a survivor on too many levels to mention, and, yet, her message isn't about HER, it's about US...you and me! It's about how the most earthshattering experience in our lives can be our soul's salvation. How can a person wrap their head around devastation and death and come out the other side to find forgiveness, love and purpose? Well, I guess you'll just have to read the book to know...

Melinda Lee Foster,
Author, Host, Spokesperson

Susie Levan has transformed her trauma into action. She lives and breathes with gratitude and forgiveness, knowing them as gifts that come with loss, pain and suffering. There is no other woman I know on this planet who so lovingly and unconditionally gives of herself to inspire others, especially women, to be fearless and to fulfill their soul's purpose.

I have known and worked side by side with Susie Levan for over a decade and can unequivocally attest to her carrying a unique and special light and love that clearly, is from heaven above. She has truly accessed the depths of her soul and lives as an extraordinary woman —who deeply touches and indelibly inspires everyone she meets.

Liz Sterling
Author, Broadcaster, Motivational Speaker and Blogger

The path of spiritual growth and enlightenment is deeply personal, often beginning unintentionally, and with no understanding of where it will lead. Susie Levan's unique awakening began with a terrifying event which turned her world upside down and left her doubting what she knew and challenged her to trust what she did not fully understand. In her book, Susie shares her ongoing journey with courage, candor, and the understanding that every experience God gives us, every person He puts in our lives, is the perfect preparation for the future that only He can see.

Susan D. McGregor, CEO
Belissima Fine Art Services

I had the great fortune of meeting Susie when my consulting business was just getting started many years ago. I was a guest speaker at an event, and Susie approached me after my talk and said to me that I had great energy and asked what she could do to assist me. Since that time Susie has helped me personally as well as my consulting business in more ways than I could have ever imagined. She has been my trusted mentor, coach, and invaluable advisor. As a consultant for some of the world's most prestigious organizations and an executive coach to highly successful executives, Susie has been my go-to coach.

She is such a special person who generously shares her priceless business and life lessons to those who know her. She simply makes the world a better place, and I will be eternally grateful for having Susie as my mentor, coach and cherished friend. In *Getting to Forgiveness*, she shares her wisdom and messages to help us remember our soul.

Patricia D. Sadar, CEO
People2Strategy

To express in words the immeasurable totality of all that I have learned from Susie Levan, may take many pages. Before I started attending Susie's Women's Wisdom Circle, I felt overwhelmed by the magnitude of personal and professional responsibilities that I had in my life. After participating in several of her workshops and bi-weekly group coaching sessions, I saw my life changing and progressively growing free from anxiety and stress while being able to focus on the issues that needed to be resolved, effortlessly.

I hired her to become my personal Life Coach. Through her wisdom and guidance, I was able to make major life decisions that allowed me to continue to grow and evolve in every aspect of my life. She is a remarkable spiritual teacher that has impacted my life in an innumerable number of ways. Her guidance and support have profoundly affected my personal spiritual growth, vibrant health and inner peace. In her book, *Getting to Forgiveness*, you will discover how to awaken to your highest potential and access the strength, love, and wisdom found within your soul.

Marta M. Sastre, CLU
Regional Sales Coordinator
AFLAC

Getting to Forgiveness shares Levan's story of courage and strength in a way that each of us can relate. From her near-death experience to her struggle with post-traumatic stress, Levan offers hope and a path toward personal growth. As someone who has empowered other women during her journey through life, Levan encourages readers to be fearless in finding their soul's purpose as she has done. This insightful memoir leaves readers equipped with the inner strength to forgive and the inspiration to find fulfillment.

Cindy Krischer Goodman
Journalist

There is only one Susie Levan. Her work is transformational, empowering and life changing. Susie has the unique ability to help people see their future by redirecting their thoughts. Susie's NDE gave her insight unto a world most have never experienced. The first time I heard her speak I had chill bumps up and down my spine. I knew that her ability to communicate and heal others was a gift that was bestowed upon her. She healed me from my own darkness and led me to the light. This book will change lives and patterns of how people view themselves and everyone in their universe. You will not be able to put it down.

Julie Saumsiegle
Blogger, Fellow Traveler

As Susie reminds us no one leaves the planet unscathed. This book insightfully describes her journey for self-discovery, while gently inspiring us to take on new challenges while digging deeper to conquer our own fears and self-doubt. As you begin to read you will hear a soft, sweet voice that speaks to you intimately about taking the journey towards believing in yourself. Susie lovingly reminds us that we are never alone on our pathway to enlightenment, love and inner joy.

Dina Bellows-Levine CPA, CFE, CFF
Bellows Associates P.A.

Getting to Forgiveness is one of those books you will read over -and over-again. Starts out with a tragic experience that you usually see only in movies, that Susie Levan transforms into a life-changing, inspirational, spiritual, and metaphoric journey for herself and her daughter, and then pays it forward to others for 31 years and running. Susie Levan taught her daughter to LIVE as if she is going to die tomorrow and, LEARN as if she is going to live forever. Through Susie, Lauren lives forever, especially in her teachings, that started on that horrific but miraculous December day in 1988. A must read!

Cindy Kushner, Tax Partner
Crowe LLP

From the moment I first met Susie Levan, 10 years ago, I knew she was extraordinary. I saw the strong, confident, and well put together woman she presented on the outside but more importantly, I sensed an inner strength that drew me in and made me want to know her more. It is said that it takes courage to walk through this life. Susie shares her courage and shear grit in her uniquely personal book, *Getting to Forgiveness.*

This work is brave, its honest and it is transforming. Her experiences would have crippled the strongest amongst us, but Susie has instead allowed them to transform her. I am honored to call Susie my friend and hope that by reading and sharing in her incredible story we will all learn to walk with courage and grace as Susie continues to do each day.

Cathy Donnelly
Director—Community Relations
Castle Group

Very few are chosen to enlighten the path of humanity in a meaningful way. Susie is a living example of the even fewer who have accepted this calling. Her loving, giving nature, her fierce determination to win over life's obstacles, her indisputable resilience, and the powerful wisdom bestowed upon her from above, are her trademarks in each chapter of this book. Her message is profound, impactful, thought provoking and divinely crafted to inspire and ignite one's purpose in life. It has been an honor to know her and to partake some of life's experience together. Susie is a true blessing in my life and in the lives of countless others.

The path to forgiveness is a road less traveled; but she reveals how this path leads travelers to true freedom. I wholeheartedly recommend this book to anyone that seeks spiritual and personal growth. The lessons are a divine revelation of what it takes to undergo a real transformation; emerging from darkness and allowing one's soul to be awaken for the true meaning of life. May the journey of forgiveness, peace and freedom begin, for each reader of this life-changing book!

Giselle Cheminand
President and CEO
GCI Worldwide Corporation

Susie Levan in her book, *Getting to Forgiveness* cracks open her heart and soul through impeccable and powerful story telling. In a pivotal instant she reviews her life and determines that there is a need for a change in her journey. Sharing her knowledge and experiences, Susie leads you to exploring your own untapped spiritual strengths by using her sensitive writing style. Anyone who needs to forgive, experiencing trauma or transition of any kind, should read this book.

Maria Soldani, Principal
Soldani Consultants

Getting to Forgiveness is a book of love and loss, of an awakening, a quest and journey on the road of life where Susie, through her unique and soulful perspective, shares wisdom and understanding with the reader. This knowledge helps and inspires the reader along their own life's path. It teaches the lesson that we are spiritual beings having a human experience. That the human experience has many obstacles which are initially experienced as "bad" or "sad" in time, unfold into lessons that nourish the soul when viewed from the correct perspective. Thank you, Susie for sharing your experiences, insights and wisdom.

Eric Radzwill, OD

Hopefully none of us will have to live through anything like the kidnapping and near-death experience that has long defined and reconstituted Susie Levan's life. Her book, *Getting to Forgiveness* is a powerful reminder that each of us already possesses the passion, strength, vision, and love required to live rich, productive, and joyful lives, if we are fearless in our efforts to do so. This is an important book about perspective and courage; Susie shares her unique, heartfelt insight into those topics masterfully.

Dorothy Klein
Executive Director
Broward Public Library Foundation

Susie's awareness and desire to evaluate her life's experiences reads like a fascinating novel--only it is her true life's story. Her personal authenticity and teaching of loving, honoring and forgiving ourselves and others is a course study for any person at any stage in their life. A must read for anyone who truly desires to know how to understand that all things that happen are steps to becoming your authentic self. Susie teaches with real life experiences—her life experiences—in a spellbinding, practical way.

Kimberly Barbar
Senior Vice President
Stiles Realty

Getting to Forgiveness shares a powerful and inspirational journey of a woman who has touched and enriched so many lives. I have known, admired, and loved Susie Levan for more than 15 years, seeing her in action with *Balance* magazine workshops, leading community projects, and supporting women seeking growth and change. She is a role model, a change agent, a beacon of light and a very special soul. To be in her company is to be savored. Her story brings raw and difficult situations to a place we first find commonality and then through lessons we find comfort, forgiveness, healing and strength.

Jennifer O'Flannery Anderson, Ph.D.

We spend most – if not all – of our life in the process of discovery. What is the meaning of our individual and collective existence? What kind of life should I live? The answers lead some of us to live intentional lives that align with our values. Others live without thought. Susie's life has been anything but unintentional. A near-death experience followed by PTSD and extraordinary pain led her on a path to find peace and goodness. It saved her life. None of us escapes the pain of existence but all of us can learn from Susie's extraordinary journey. Our answers may differ, but her key discoveries of how love, forgiveness and reflection can heal the soul are universal.

Josie Bacallao
Nonprofit Executive and Fellow Traveler

Susie is a person I admire who has offered counsel and wisdom to many of us traveling through life. She brings a unique perspective sharing her wisdom of how she coped through a near-death experience and through that came out a stronger woman. She has motivated and inspired us to be better women by truly taking care of ourselves in mind, body, and spirit. We will all take away some great tips from her insights in her book, *Getting to Forgiveness*.

Maureen Shea
CEO, Florida/Caribbean
Right Management

Susie Levan has taught me that forgiveness, especially self-forgiveness, is essential for spiritual growth. Susie empowers us to let go of the past so that we may heal, find peace and reframe our inner narrative to move forward. Through *Getting to Forgiveness*, Susie provides a compassionate and helping hand through the journey of recovery, discovery and awakening.

Nancy Thies
Nonprofit Executive

Long before the Near-Death Experience described in her book, Susie Levan was already a special and unique person. At a time when women were still expected to either stay at home, or work in 'lady' jobs, Susie defied convention and expectations, parlaying a starting secretarial position into an on-the-job business education that ultimately led her to become COO of a major NYSE-listed holding company.

After her NDE, the same drive and skills that she had used to succeed in the business world served to help her overcome extreme trauma and turn her attention outward toward helping others. If spirituality was a 'company', she would once again be COO.

Susie Levan has explored all areas of human and divine spirituality, and has made it her life mission to share her knowledge and to teach others to find themselves, to find peace within, to find ways to give back, and to find forgiveness for the many hurts we experience throughout life—no matter how charmed that life may seem from the outside. The magic that sets her apart is her pure kindness. She gives, comforts, teaches and mentors, expecting nothing in return. Her reward is in seeing someone grow and love being alive.

Getting to Forgiveness is an extension of her own life and soul. What she has brought to others through her work as Founder and Publisher of *Balance* magazine, and leader of self-development workshops and the Women's Wisdom Circle, she brings to the pages of this book, in the most personal way—sharing her own challenges in overcoming trauma that she has not previously revealed, and that one would never expect her to have experienced based on meeting her as she is today. You will be moved by her story, touched by her revelations, and profoundly transformed by the love and insight she pours into each page.

Ellen Jaffe
On-Air Host / Community Affairs Host
Easy 93.1 WFEZ

GETTING TO
FORGIVENESS

SUSIE LEVAN

FOREWORD BY GLORIA ESTEFAN

GETTING TO
FORGIVENESS

*What A Near-Death Experience Can
Teach Us About Loss, Resilience and Love*

Bee Hive
PUBLISHING

Although the author and publisher have made every effort to ensure the accuracy and completeness of information contained in this book, we assume no responsibility for errors, inaccuracies, omissions, or any inconsistency herein.

Library of Congress has cataloged the hardcover edition as follows:
Names: Levan, Susie, author.
Title: Getting to Forgiveness: What A Near-Death Experience Can Teach Us About Loss, Resilience and Love
Description: First (edition) Florida: Bee Hive Publishing, 2019
Identifiers: ISBN 978-1-949639-65-0, 978-1-949639-94-0 LCCN 2019912578
Subjects: Near-Death Experience, Meditation, Spirituality

Published by Bee Hive Publishing
Manufactured and printed in the United States of America
First Edition
Jacket Design by George Stevens

*This book is dedicated to the memory of
our beautiful daughter, Lauren.*

CONTENTS

FOREWORD

I like to think I know a thing or two about stepping Into the Light. It was the name of my world tour in 1991, following a serious tour bus accident on an icy mountain road the previous year. Parts of me were damaged—specifically my vertebrae—and I ended up with two titanium rods in my back. During the long, hard road to recovery, with family and friends helping to lift me up, I knew that my back may have been broken, but my spirit, though shaken, ultimately was not. It's interesting what happens inside of you—the strength you find—when you survive something that could and maybe should have killed you. Your life is never the same. You gain a new perspective. You live with a kind of gratitude for ordinary days you never had before.

I met Susie Levan in 2001, when she'd experienced her own tragedy that had changed her life. She'd reached out to me for an interview and to appear on the cover of her magazine, *Living in Balance* (later *Balance* magazine). Both of us were born in Cuba and had moved to Miami as toddlers. Our families worked long, often grueling hours as laborers—grateful for the opportunity to make a life in this country no matter what it took. As fate would have it, our paths had crossed as teenagers, though we never officially met, when I fronted a local band that entertained at some of the parties Susie attended.

When we connected in 2001 for the magazine, I learned Susie was a former corporate executive. She'd barely survived a kidnapping thirteen years earlier when she and her seven-year-old daughter spent hours in the sweltering trunk of a car. Susie emerged from a near-death experience as a result of all that with part of her broken— though for her it wasn't her back but her spirit. It took years, but she learned how to embrace the posttraumatic stress that had resulted and to channel all that happened into empowering other women to overcome trauma and significant life challenges.

After my accident, to get myself through intense back surgery and will myself to heal, I discovered a kind of self-discipline and resiliency I never knew existed. Like Susie, I believe each of us possesses the ability to heal ourselves. It may involve help from another— sometimes it even takes a village—but ultimately it is up to us, individually, and I know from my own experience that we do have it in us.

As a little girl I was keenly aware of energy and vibrations around me—a more spiritual component of life—and to this day I trust my instincts as much or even more than logic. With that, all of it needs to factor into making the right choices for ourselves. As human beings we function on different levels, though we may not always be aware of it. Susie and I share the conviction that an abundance of lessons must be learned while we are here in the physical body. Our experiences can range from the highest of highs to unimaginable lows that result from trauma and tragedy. While the pain may seem unbearable, if we are fearless enough to be introspective and honest, it helps us gain a more profound appreciation for the happy times.

No one says avoiding giving energy to negative thoughts isn't hard, but on a grander scale, each of us contributes to the thoughts that make up the world. These thoughts lead to actions, and events follow—personal and global events. I believe if we understand how responsible each of us is for the world we create, we can more easily solve our problems and attain what we desire. It comes back to what's inside of us—what's available to us—and uncovering this is the first step.

I am grateful to Susie Levan for the opportunity to have met her when I did. I am especially grateful for the fact that despite going to a place from which she may never have recovered, she has written this book, chronicling that time, to help others find their own resilience and their own path.

Gloria Estefan

Multiple Grammy Award Winner
Humanitarian and Philanthropist

PROLOGUE

There came a time when the risk to remain tight in the bud
was more painful than the risk it took to blossom.

ANAÏS NIN

Some years ago, I had an idea to write a book. The truth, though, is that I never really thought about it until people suggested my life story was worth reading. They kept encouraging me to do it, so the idea took root. In retrospect, others must have seen what I didn't, and I am forever grateful. As a reluctant writer, the opportunity for me to deeply reflect, analyze, share, and write as candidly as I know how has been a gift I can only hope will inspire others to move fearlessly ahead in their own lives ... to live a full and empowered existence. I hope my experiences light the way for you.

It's no accident that the title of the book is *Getting to Forgiveness*, as you will read it is something that has been calling out to you. I humbly come from a place of personal knowing and experiences that have shaped who I am. Writing my book has truly been gut wrenching at times and a deeply cathartic, transforming experience. It's possible you found your way here because of the title of this book, or because you are seeking to forgive yourself or others, or you're looking for healing or balance or a way to return to a time when you felt comfortable in your life—or perhaps you are looking to feel that way for the first time. Many, if not most, of us go through some form of illness (our own and/or that of a loved one) or maybe divorce, depression, anxiety, loss, mental or physical abuse, grief, and other significant and unimaginable challenges. None of us get out alive. I've heard it said that no one leaves the planet unscathed in some form or another. We are all navigating some sort of crisis at different times in our life. What I've learned is that, in order to heal, grow, and change, we need to open our heart for us to fully awaken. We all need to figure out what the healing path looks like for us individually and then have the courage to follow it. It took me a long time to do that, and though I've learned so much along the way, the fact is, I'm still a work in progress and forever will be. Healing and growing never end. They teach us how to embrace uncertainty, and they inspire and teach us to change to truly live and love.

For me, a series of life events—including my own near-death experience (NDE) following a kidnapping, where my young daughter, Lauren, and I were forced into the hot trunk of a car in 1988—brought me to my knees … and eventually to write this book. I began writing it less than a year before Lauren's untimely passing from cancer at the age of thirty-six, in September of 2018, which further helped to define what I would ultimately say. The loss of my beautiful LP, as we called her, left me unhinged, disjointed, disconnected, and filled with immense grief, sheer exhaustion, chaos, and despair. Even though I believe in an afterlife and had been to the "other side," I was full of holes and questions—reopening old wounds and creating brand new ones. I felt overwhelmed and debilitated; at that moment, I was reminded again how (most of) the things that I used to worry about really don't matter. As Richard Carlson, PhD, wrote, "Don't sweat the small stuff—it's all small stuff"—teaching us how to put life and challenges in perspective. And boy, was he right!

My search for answers about all of this, what that search and journey revealed, and what I anticipate will continue to be revealed is, in my opinion, a powerful reason for a book—and maybe a learning tool for you. I hope you will find the way to a more meaningful and happier life, despite all of the challenges you may have gone through and continue to face. My intention and hope for this book is to help you uncover, illuminate, plant a seed, and guide you through your own journey.

There are obstacles and unexpected, defining moments in each of our lives. These can shove us hard down dark, foreboding paths until we arrive at the point where we are left with no choice but to confront more than we ever thought we would about ourselves—and until we enter a realm of greater understanding. I believe that if we don't embrace that journey, what is the point in being alive?

I grew up in the 1950s and 1960s in a Latin culture that—perhaps because of the kind of intense tradition we observed and the long hours involved in working laboriously hard jobs just to survive—left little time for self-examination and reflection. The thought of finding out what "made someone tick," let alone what made me tick, was nowhere to be found in the (cultural) cerebral cortex—that part of the brain responsible for higher thought. That is not to say there aren't many extraordinarily intelligent and talented people given to higher thought in my culture; there most certainly are! My father, whom I admired and adored, for example, was a voracious reader almost to the day he died. Except for finishing high school in Cuba, he lacked a formal education, but because of what he continuously read, absorbed, and processed the way he did, he could talk with anyone about anything. In the week he passed away, he'd been devouring a book on Nikola Tesla, engaging us in discourse about the inventor's futuristic pursuits until my father's last hours in hospice care.

Despite his knowledge, my father's more conservative, often limited, blinding, and inflexible ways of moving through the world (he was definitely a product of the beliefs and constraints of his culture and generation) had extremely negative repercussions on my adolescent life, including my being forced into a stifling early marriage, creating an intense anger and distrust toward my dad. But at one point, many years later, he encouraged me to attend Silva Mind Control classes with him. Popular in the 1960s and 1970s, what is now called the Silva Method purports to increase and sustain optimal mental function ... by some unconventional methods. We had grown apart because of my crippling feelings of betrayal toward him, and I was surprised about all of it: the invitation and the fact that he was interested in such an expansive pursuit. I also learned at that time that he'd been reading books on spirituality and metaphysics. I went with him, and I will never forget having the opportunity to sit with my father as we shared new fascinating concepts and meditations of the mind's hidden potential in those many weeks and months taking the course together. They taught us to master our mind. He and I were naturals in visualizing and meditation, manifesting a true forgiveness and healing for us both by the end of the program. The depths of his curiosity and intellect inspire me to this day.

When I decided to write my story, my journey had taken me from the top of a steep corporate ladder, where I'd ended up as COO of a major holding company, to near death in the trunk of a car, to a mental, physical, and spiritual breakdown out of which it had taken me a long time to climb. I never thought I would become a nondenominational pastoral counselor, Life Coach, hypnotherapist, teacher of metaphysics, teacher of meditation, or a Reiki master. But that's where my path took me—and a lot of other places as well.

When I finally resiliently emerged from my darkest abyss, and when I'd harnessed and synthesized all of my experiences and put them to work helping others in crisis to embrace their truth and to help them find balance and equanimity, I thought that was a reason for a book.

My wish is that sharing my experiences and lessons with you will stir your soul and will help guide, illuminate, and empower you to make your journey a little smoother.

Love and light,

Susie Levan

October 2019
Fort Lauderdale, Florida

CHAPTER 1

"DOES MY LIFE END TODAY?" ENCOUNTERS AND MIRACLES

The tragedy of life is not that it ends so soon,
but that we wait so long to begin it.

W. M. LEWIS

I t was pitch black, exceedingly hot, and my child and I were suffocating. All I could hear when we'd started out was the clippity-clop of the little metal warning tabs a car makes contact with as it speeds along the highway but doesn't stay in its lane. We were obviously being driven all over the road. As long as the car had been moving, we'd see occasional light from the back of the brake lights and could feel a rush of air coming up from the underside, feeding into the trunk. But the car had stopped and been turned off some time ago. It was 1988, and internal trunk latches were a thing of the future. There was no way out. This was not the way I'd envisioned dying. In fact, in your thirties, who thinks much about death at all?

I don't know how long we'd been riding, because the night before, when Alan and I had come home late following a management meeting at the bank, they'd already gotten into the house. Three disguised men had secured our seven-year-old daughter, Lauren (from my previous marriage), and housekeeper, Petrona, in an upstairs bedroom, forced us at gunpoint to lie face down on the living room floor, and removed our jewelry and watches. So I had no way of telling time in the trunk. The fact is, it probably didn't matter.

The night before had been very long. Earlier that evening I'd made my customary 6:00 p.m. phone call to Petrona, the one I always made when I could not be with my daughter to check on her dinner and bath, and certainly to speak with my child. When I called, Petrona's answers to all my questions were stilted and largely one-word responses. It was a very odd call with someone who'd essentially been a part of our family since Lauren was four months old. I'd not been allowed to speak with Lauren, being told she was upstairs asleep.

"What do you mean asleep?" I'd asked urgently. "Is she ill?"

Petrona said she was not sick, but she'd not been forthcoming about much else. I knew something was wrong, and it plagued me throughout the management meeting. I could not wait to drive back with Alan, even entertaining the idea of leaving before the meeting was over, but we had come in the same car.

When we'd arrived home, all the exterior and interior lights were off, which they never are, and my instincts were on fire. I couldn't shake my gut feeling—call it mother's intuition. I was standing behind Alan when he put the key in the lock and opened the door, and one of the perpetrators grabbed him by the wrist to pull him inside. I took off, flying down the very steep driveway, kicking off my heels in the process. I screamed as loudly as possible (hoping a neighbor would hear me), but one of the men in the house had sprinted after me and grabbed me by the hair, dragging me all the way back up the ridge.

Eventually Alan and I were put into Lauren's bedroom with her and Petrona, where we were ordered to remain until the next day. We were told we'd be awoken to carry out the actions the perpetrators had planned. Fortunately Lauren slept, shielded by us from the unimaginable reality of what was happening and what might happen. I slept by her in her bed, my arms wrapped around her like a safe, warm cocoon. But it was a lie. I knew I could not protect her. The powerlessness that comes over you as a parent at a time like that is indescribable. The minutes ticked by like years, and I remember feeling that as long a night as it was, I hoped the dawn would never come. But it did.

Despite the terror I felt for myself and my family, somehow I'd maintained enough presence of mind to pay very close attention to these criminals—to scrutinize them, in fact. If I lived, I knew I would need to provide detailed descriptions to the police, and I was intent on doing so.

All three of the perpetrators wore trucker's caps and wigs as well as sunglasses and gloves. And while I couldn't explain why, one of the perpetrators was dressed entirely in blue (a sweat suit); another in red (also a sweat suit); and the other, the leader or mastermind, in white, including a white windbreaker. I don't know why, but I also noticed their shoes and in what hand they held their guns. After we'd been taken from Lauren's bedroom around dawn, Alan and I were told to shower in the master bathroom as if preparing for a typical day. As I passed by the bed to get there, the mastermind—dressed in white—sat on the side of the bed, talking on the phone. I observed that because his wig added a layer between him and the receiver, he was holding the receiver slightly away from his ear, to the extent that I could discern a woman's voice on the other end. Additionally, he had removed his gloves, which revealed alabaster-like skin. I determined he was an albino; possibly he thought wearing white clothing made the absence of pigment in his skin less obvious—less of a contrast.

After showering, Lauren and I had been forced into the trunk of Alan's car, and at the crack of dawn, we'd been driven off. Alan was taken to the bank by the mastermind in my two-seater Mercedes SL, nearly an hour away in Fort Lauderdale, where he'd been instructed to remove the contents of the vault, stuff it into a suitcase, exit the bank, and return to the parking lot, where the mastermind would be waiting for it behind the wheel.

None of us knew until the last second that Lauren and I would end up in this trunk rather than wait at home as hostages with one or two of the gunmen. Our ultimate destination had not been disclosed, although we were given the "reassurance" that if the crime were successfully executed—meaning if the authorities were not alerted in the process—Alan would receive a call about our location.

It felt as though Lauren and I were suspended in the space between life and death. We could have been in that trunk thirty minutes or three hours at that point; I just didn't know. What I did know was that I could not let my child come to this kind of end. What if she never knew what gifts she had and how she would use them in the world? God could take me, but not her, and I prayed while telling Him just that. I was familiar with Psalm 23, as I'd heard it recited at funerals. During a conversion to Judaism, which I talk about later in the book, I studied it, believing it to be quite powerful and soothing. In time it would come to have even more significance in my life.

Lauren stirred and said she had to go to the bathroom. I told her just to go ahead and do it, though she was always a strong child and resisted what she decided would embarrass her. Later she said she was hungry and was done with the game—hide-and-go-seek—which I'd told her we were playing when the perpetrators had ordered us into the trunk. I made up silly little stories and sang her songs to stall and entertain her, not even knowing what I was saying, always holding her close.

"Just be patient. I'm sure Alan will find us soon," I lied, clawing at some faith, hoping against hope that he would. *Has the robbery taken place? Is my husband still alive?* I couldn't allow the crushing feelings that thought raised to overwhelm me; every ounce of energy had to go into keeping Lauren alive. In retrospect, maybe *sangfroid*— composure in danger or under trying circumstances—is a good word to describe my state. Perhaps plain old *numbness* is another good word.

I'm not sure where it came from, but I told Lauren that Mommy hadn't slept much last night and asked if she wanted to join me in a nap. I encouraged her to relax and close her eyes. Right away she said yes, that she would—my wondrous child, not resisting no matter how uncomfortable she felt. Though I didn't dwell on spiritual ideas at that time in my life, I knew she was a blessing. She had been born to me after a long period of time when I'd been told I would have no more children. I could not lose her like this. I heard her breathing change as she drifted off. I listened intently, wondering if the sound would soon stop as I'd hear her take her very last breath.

✸

I was COO and executive vice president of a New York Stock Exchange–listed corporation. I was the quintessential career corporate soldier and type-A personality. I was disciplined, dedicated, dogmatic, and relentless about work, and I prided myself on my executive cool that complemented my array of stylish but no-nonsense petite-sized suits. I ate, drank, slept, and breathed business and, in addition to logging years of exceedingly hard work, embraced the twists and turns my life had taken to get me to this point. In many respects, life had been hard, but I knew I was harder.

Alan had the black belt in all things business, but I also had prowess in the areas in which I worked. I could fix it, solve it, organize it, and execute it, often when others could not. I could make it happen. But in this moment, none of it mattered. My track record could not help us now. Everything had been stripped away. We were entirely at someone else's mercy—someone I could no longer even see—stuffed into a moving (or no longer moving) metal casket. I thought about my parents. I thought about my older daughter, Gina, who lived in Miami Beach. I thought about relatives and friends who loved and nurtured me whenever I needed them and whom I loved dearly. I thought about Alan's three children. If this was to be Lauren's and my last day on earth, there were things I needed to say to every one of these people. I wanted to be able to thank them and comfort them—all of them. What goes through your head when death looms fast and large is like nothing you've ever known in your life. When you believe you have hours or maybe just minutes to live, perspective becomes laser focused. I can tell you from experience it's not a cliché that the things that consumed you at work or in your personal life fall away, and all that's left in your mind, your heart, and your soul are profound thoughts of the people you love.

Twenty years earlier, at eighteen years of age and in the throes of a difficult marriage I'd never wanted in the first place, I'd gotten out of the house by taking a job as a real estate secretary. After two other jobs, I moved on to another company, and as that company grew and evolved, it acquired a bank. I'd worked very hard and had the good fortune of going along for an incredible ride, just three months ago marrying Alan, who'd become chairman and CEO of the bank. This man was as kind and loving as he was courageous. He'd argued with the gunmen about not putting us in the trunk, a tactic that turned bad and could have gotten him killed, so he negotiated for at least a pillow for our heads and ended up getting one. Because of this man, in our darkest hour, we had a soft place to fall.

Alan and I had worked together, with a few other highly trusted individuals, to soldier through unimaginable business and personal edge-of-your-seat challenges, gains, and losses. Between us we'd had three marriages and divorces. We'd finally realized we belonged together on every level. We'd taken the five children in our blended family (plus their friends—honeymoon for twelve!) to Marco Island on Florida's west coast the weekend we were married, just three months earlier. Forty-eight hours from now, we were scheduled to take our children on a family ski trip to Colorado. So I wondered what was being asked of me here: to accept that it was all going to end today ... like this?

The news reports that many Florida crime victims end up in the Everglades. When the car stopped, I thought we might have been driven there, our bones left to bake through the scorching metal, to be discovered only if the car were ever found. I straddled the line between indescribable sadness and protective mode—whatever I could muster of it—for Lauren.

It turned out I didn't have to wait long for an answer to my question about dying. It came during my recitation of Psalm 23.

The Lord is my shepherd; I shall not want.

He maketh me to lie down in green pastures:
he leadeth me beside the still waters.

He restoreth my soul: he leadeth me in the paths
of righteousness for his name's sake.

Yea, though I walk through the valley of the shadow of death, I will fear
no evil: for thou art with me; thy rod and thy staff they comfort me.

Thou preparest a table before me in the presence of mine enemies:
thou anointest my head with oil; my cup runneth over.

Surely goodness and mercy shall follow me all the days of my
life: and I will dwell in the house of the Lord forever. Amen.

I implored God to take me, not my daughter. I said the word *amen*, and at that moment, I felt something pulling me from my physical body, out through the top of my head, at an unfathomable speed. It was a *whoosh*—like the whoosh of air under the car as it had sped along the highway with us in the trunk, only a million times more intense.

I was a businessperson. I'd managed people and whole departments. I was logical and methodical—all left brain. But what was happening confounded me, as I could neither categorize it nor put it in a box or column. I could not make sense of it, and the thing is, I didn't want to. At that moment I had no fear and no anxiety. I felt a pervading sense of peace and calm, a high I wanted forever. I was never one for drugs, but I thought this was what it must feel like.

My eyes had been closed, and I opened them slowly as a brilliant, unearthly light revealed itself to me. Since that time, I've tried over and over to explain this—the incomprehensible largeness of it all—but there really are no words. Also since that time, I've read that on his deathbed, when he was slipping into his final moments, Apple founder, chairman, and CEO Steve Jobs had uttered the words, "OH WOW. OH WOW. OH WOW," as mentioned in his sister's eulogy.[1] She wrote them all in uppercase presumably to emphasize the exuberance he'd expressed behind them. Maybe that's what I can say here too. That's what I was experiencing—wherever I was.

The light was brilliant. Yet when I opened my eyes, it did not hurt them the way staring into the sun might. I could see I was traveling through a tunnel, my mind going a million miles a minute, watching and relishing. At the same time, I was totally confused. A portal with a shimmering, silvery glow appeared, and I was engulfed in all of its light. Strangely, the light had energy—it had feeling and emotion to it. The only word I can use to describe it is love. It felt safe, as though I were an embryo floating in a warm, serene space enveloped by unconditional love. There were sounds, music, and a kind of majestic energy that was without boundaries. To this day I cannot accurately or fully describe what was happening to me. The spiritual revelation is far beyond anything we know in this life—far beyond comprehension.

At some point, with all of this, I knew I was surrounded by something else. I have no words or descriptions for them other than light-filled presences. Light and energy emanated from them to me, providing a sense of joy, peace, and always love. It was euphoric. Since

---

1   Christopher John Farley, "'Oh Wow': What Do Steve Jobs's Last Words Really Mean?" October 31, 2011, https://blogs.wsj.com/speakeasy/2011/10/31/oh-wow-what-do-steve-jobss-last-words-really-mean/.

then I've sometimes thought of them as guides or angelic beings, certainly otherworldly, and I knew they were there to take care of me.

To my right I felt an incredibly huge presence, what I came to call a warrior angel. That's what he looked like, though in a sense the beings around me were all formless—like clouds. I looked into the warrior angel's eyes, and he looked into mine—but the thing is, I can't really say if I was looking directly into his eyes or into something cloud-like there ... maybe a form of energy. He told me he was the archangel Michael, that he was a supreme protector, and that he'd been watching over me for many lifetimes.

My life as I'd known it had been upended at that point. I no longer felt the urge or need to make sense of any of this—to question, challenge, doubt, force, or look for reasons. It just was. I was absorbing all of it without concern—without what would normally have impelled me to dissect and analyze it. I was very comfortable. I didn't understand what was going on, but it no longer mattered. I felt a heightened sense of awareness, and then the question about my death came to mind.

"Am I dead?" I asked. "Is this heaven? Where am I?" I felt myself just thinking that thought.

While no one actually spoke, they communicated with me telepathically, and I found I could receive it. I was told I was in a different realm, a different dimension, where veils had been lifted. I was, to use a popular phrase, on the other side. But no, I was not dead.

I asked about my daughter, wondering if she was there with me, and they told me to look down, where I could see her sound asleep in the trunk. I was still in there too—my physical body—my arms around her as we lay together in fetal position.

When my thoughts went to Alan, I was telepathically directed to something I can only characterize as a little movie, where they showed me what he was doing in the bank. I could see him moving about frantically, trying to explain to the bank president that the clock was ticking on his wife and daughter who were hostages in a trunk, imploring the president to get the keys and lead him to the safe. I saw him filling the suitcase with thousands and thousands of dollars. I could feel his anxiety, his worry, his fear, his heavy heart. I felt everything he was feeling at that moment as though we were the same person. I felt a powerful connection to my husband and tried to determine if I could get a message to him. But I could not.

Next, I was given a life review: a movie of my own life on a big white screen. I was able to see people I loved, people I'd hurt, people I'd touched in various ways. Everything I'd done in my life up to that moment, I reexperienced. I could feel the depth and scope of everyone's feelings in addition to mine.

The irony was, while I did not know it at the time and wouldn't understand it until much later, no judgment was going on among these beings. No punishment. It was a personal soul growth and shift I needed to see and feel. That's what they wanted. I would come to learn that I needed an awakening of sorts in order to go back into my current realm and, because of my life review, life as a different person. I had to release and forgive others for whatever they had done to me—and clearly to release and forgive myself. Everything is connected, and everything is part of each of us. I'd been carrying this sandbag of hurt, pain, resentment, negativity, and lack of forgiveness around all my life. Understanding how what we do to others—in whatever form, big or small—hurts both the person to whom it is done and also the person who is doing it was a powerful lesson I needed to learn.

There are just no words to describe the power and potential of what was happening to me. I was reeling and gleaming with a new inner light. I knew that we come to earth in a physical body *only* to serve one another and to love, and the single emotion we take with us when we die is love.

Up to that point I had always been a "doing" person. My life was defined by ticking off tasks on behemoth to-do lists. It was strictly about pursuits, goals, objectives, competition, and achievements—and maybe about not being left behind. Though I wouldn't go back to my physical body with an immediate understanding and appreciation of the fact that I now needed to become a "being" person, the idea would come in time. I didn't quite know what I'd been given that day, but it would be there for me when I was ready for it. Today wasn't my time to die: in fact, it was my time to live.

One of the primary messages I was being given was to raise my vibration—my frequency—as a way to receive information. I would come to know that this is done through meditation. Meditation is a muscle that we need to practice with, use, and build up, and the means to do so had been given to me in that experience.

I was going back to the side from which I'd come, armed with a message of love in everything. As simple as the phrase sounds, echoed for centuries by poets and musicians, love is all there is—though it's actually a highly complex concept when we try to apply it to our own lives.

In time I'd realize all of this had been knocking at my door for ages. I'd be in bookstores, drawn to what was then called the occult section (fortunately this topic now has a better moniker; a few, in fact, all under the titles of metaphysics, spirituality, or New Age), and I'd sometimes go there, feeling a strong pull. I didn't understand it, and I often chose to ignore it, so the universe has a way of getting our attention, leaving us no other choice. I was having a near-death experience, and I don't know of a better way to get someone's attention than that.

MIRACLE OF MIRACLES

It was now time for me to return. I felt I'd been given a light-filled goodbye hug. I was speeding back into my physical body. The tunnel was reversed, and as fast as I'd gone up, I was coming down. I was headed backward, and as I think about it now, I can still hear the whooshing sounds. I had no idea how much time had elapsed—how long I'd been with these divine beings of light. There was a very loud sound, like a thump—and a thud—and I was back in my body. I must have moved—jerked, even—because Lauren awoke.

"Look, Mommy," she said as she opened her eyes, pointing up. "There's a hole in the trunk."

I turned my head and opened and focused my eyes on the base-ball-sized opening through which cool, fresh air was now flowing. I felt oddly detached and calm. We could both see the hole, and we could breathe. We could see the bright blue sky, the clouds, the overhead telephone wires with two distinct poles. Dust particles were filtering in—just as you'd see coming through a window on a beam of sunlight. My heart soared. I wanted to put my hand through this miracle of a hole in the trunk to test what my daughter and I were seeing, but I stopped myself. As tears of joy streamed down my cheek, I told myself this was a gift from God and that I just needed to trust it. I told Lauren it must be true: Mommy had just been with God and the angels, and everything would be all right. I was feeling more at peace in the air and light that now suffused what I'd been certain, for as long as we'd been in there, would be our coffin.

In time, we heard a car pull up. I had no idea if it was Alan, the gunmen, or someone else, but I had to believe for the best. In truth, the gunmen were not really on my mind after the near-death experi-ence and miracle I'd just experienced, so I knew the car was there to help us. As it turned out, the car was driven by Alan's attorney, Alison

Miller, with Alan in the passenger seat and the bank president in the car as well. We could hear hurried footsteps making their way around to the front of the car we were in, where the latch was located to pop the trunk, and in a couple of seconds we were free. The look on Alan's face can never be replicated, and I would ever want to see it again. I could tell he thought he was unlatching his wife and daughter's tomb, wherein we lay dead of heatstroke or suffocation. But thanks to divine intervention, we were very much alive.

There were tears, hugs, and kisses, and Lauren and I proceeded to point to the hole that had saved us. But it was gone! I bent over the trunk, which was now closed, fingering the place where we'd seen it, frantically but gingerly feeling for it as though sifting for a valuable ring I'd lost in the sand. I was surprised and disappointed that I was not being allowed to show my husband the miracle that had delivered us back to him.

As the hours, days, and months (even years) passed, there was so much I wanted to share with Alan about my experience in a place that just cannot be described. But really, who could comprehend it—or even believe it? As magnificent, caring, and loving as he was, certainly not my stoic, pragmatic, Brooks Brothers–attired bank chairman and CEO husband.

In chapter 5, we will see that despite the blessings I'd received during my near-death experience, the trauma of the kidnapping would have residual effects leading to a near breakdown in the form of posttraumatic stress disorder (PTSD). But I would come out the other side understanding that in some way I really had died that day. My life as I knew it no longer existed. A new life with joyful vision and direct connection to source, filled with unconditional love, had taken its place. But what was I to do with it?

CHAPTER 2

THE AMERICAN DREAM: SACRIFICE, RISK TAKING, AND HARD WORK

Life is either a daring adventure or nothing at all.

HELEN KELLER

When I think of Cuba, I think of sugar—and anything sweet! I was born there. It's strange when you think about the trajectory of your life, because had my family remained there, my life would have been so incredibly different. I would never have had my children or have met and married the love of my life—my soul mate, Alan—and I'd never have been in the trunk of that car. I'd not have had the near-death experience that altered the course of my life forever.

Cuba is a beautiful country with spirited people. One of the most exquisite beaches in the world, Playa Varadero, looks like someone spread the pristine contents of a Texas-sized sugar bowl all along the shore. The island's rum drinks, including world-famous Mojitos, quench the thirst and sweeten the palate going down, and around the time I was born in Havana, the Spanish colonial homes in each neighborhood were painted ice cream–colored pastels. More sweets! My destiny was not to grow up in Cuba. Though I left for the United States when I was two years old, Cuba will forever be in my blood.

The country experienced a great deal of political and governmental instability and change between 1947 and 1955. Led by Fulgencio Battista, its defining casinos, hotels, and clubs including the world-famous Tropicana (all run for quite a while by the infamous US-based syndicate that included Lucky Luciano, Meyer Lansky, and Santo Trafficante Jr.), with rampant gambling (including horse racing) and prostitution, were nationalized. Economic growth occurred unevenly and was earmarked by corruption. There were strikes and an unhappy workforce all over the island. Everyone talked about the dark political climate. Cuba would never recover, and even before that was apparent, my father somehow intuitively knew something else awaited him in the United States.

In 1947, when my parents, Rafael and Sonia, got engaged, Mom was just eighteen. A friend showed them brochures about travel to the United States. The one with the Statue of Liberty really inspired them—especially my dad. Working as a plasterer's apprentice in construction, Dad was now having a hard time finding jobs and was ready for a change. Their destiny shifted with that particular brochure, as they chose New York for their 1948 honeymoon. The trip would forever change the course of their lives—and naturally mine. They immediately began saving money for their honeymoon on a Pan Am propeller plane to Miami and then to New York City—their first plane ride. While in New York, my dad, who was twenty-four and quite committed to providing for his new wife and anticipated family, was impressed with the multitude of work opportunities the United States had to offer. It was post-WWII, and construction of new homes and high-rise buildings was booming. With so much political unrest and economic uncertainty in Cuba, he decided New York was where they belonged.

Six months later they made the big move. Mom readily agreed to accompany her new, as they say, tall, dark, and handsome husband on this long-distance adventure. But she spoke little English and soon felt extremely lonely and isolated. Maybe more importantly, she was ill prepared for the characteristic gray, dreary, frigid, snowy New York winters. Long-distance phone calls within the States were expensive, let alone the cost of making international calls. The eldest of eight, she was really still a child herself, but in those times and in that culture, that was the marrying age. If you weren't married before age twenty, you were considered an old maid. She was from a close-knit, dynamic family—all as much friends as they were relations, and later I'd be blessed to be born into this warm, wonderful web of many uncles, aunts, and cousins. Now only nineteen, she was in every respect far from all that—truly far from home.

Since Mom couldn't call anyone in Cuba, she wrote long, detailed letters—every single day. Then each day she'd wait by the mailbox, hoping the mailman would bring her news from home. Barely surviving that first winter in America, she begged my father to return to sunny, balmy Havana. Dad reluctantly agreed to leave his new job and all it represented for their future to head back to Cuba, but only on the condition that they would one day return to the United States. That was the deal.

Back in Cuba, hearing her native tongue spoken everywhere and able to understand what was happening around her, feeling safe and comfortable around her family, relishing the sun on her shoulders again, Mom was happy and relaxed, soon becoming pregnant with me. She never forgot her agreement with Dad, however, to one day return to the States, and she improved her English by watching American television broadcasts and reading English books while Dad worked as a plasterer. She was joyful about being home with her family in an environment that offered familiarity and support, but there was never any doubt that she would keep her word to her husband.

A midwife delivered me at my maternal grandmother's—my *Abuela* Cuca's—house, which was the custom in Cuba in the 1950s. Of course, in those days no one knew the baby's gender in advance, so my first baby gift—wrapped and already awaiting my birth—was a toy truck. Dad had been hoping for a boy, which he would get when my brother, Peter, was born eleven years later, but he quickly fell in love with his firstborn. My family recalls his escorting me around for all to admire in my meticulously pressed linen dresses, dark wavy hair, and hair bows. As I got older, I was always Abuela Cuca's *flaquita*, or "skinny one," as opposed to others in the family, who all definitely had meat on their bones. But my father adored me no matter what I looked like, perhaps in part because he was thin himself—all his side of the family was thin! My father was soft spoken but strict. We were all afraid of his Latin temper; when he was mad, all hell broke loose—he would just give you a look, and you knew he wasn't pleased about something. He had a *machismo* style to his manner and rules—manly and self-reliant. I adored him. As I got older, we'd develop the closest of relationships; he came to depend on me as his appointed assistant project manager during ongoing meticulous kitchen and bathroom renovation projects in the many houses he moved us into over the years and subsequently flipped. We would become a great team, and I loved feeling chosen. I felt a sense of security and self-confidence when I was with him. His faith in me would become the bedrock of my life, which is why, when all that was shattered some years later (which I talk about in the next chapter), it was like a form of death to me from which I thought I'd never recover.

Dad now had a good-sized taste for living in the United States and was planning his next move. When I was a year old, he applied for a visa to return to the place he thought would be the most beneficial for his young family. However, this time it was to live at a different latitude: Miami, Florida. Liking the idea of a shorter plane ride (for easy hops back home) and tropical weather that mirrored Cuba's, Mom agreed to go to South Florida, and we left when I was two. As it turned out, we were one of the few families at that time that left prerevolution Cuba. Mom got pregnant with my twin sisters, Yolanda and Mirella—named after characters she'd adored in a French film—four years later. She returned to Cuba temporarily to give birth at home with a midwife, surrounded by her family, just as she had with me.

In Miami, Dad was a hard, conscientious worker. He would leave very early in the morning—in fact, most mornings it was still dark outside. Mom would be in the kitchen, scurrying around making his breakfast and packing his lunch. He would come into our rooms and kiss us goodbye, telling us how much he loved us. He also passionately loved his job and was always one of the first people to arrive. As a responsible and talented full-fledged union-card-carrying plasterer, he was able to work his way up to foreman, managing a big team of other plasterers for Rooney Construction, a large and prestigious construction company in Miami in those days. He was very proud of his new position. He was given a raise and a new company truck to drive, and he felt on top of the world.

Mom knew how to sew on a Singer sewing machine. My Abuela Cuca had one at her home that the family used for alterations. When the twins started elementary school, to supplement Dad's income, Mom took a sewing job in a factory, doing the finish work on various garments. She would come home hot and tired but filled with stories of the hundreds of garments she'd sewn that day on a coveted top-of-the-line Merrow. She was quite competitive with the other seam-stresses, and her powerful work ethic, along with that of my dad, was something I would emulate from the time I was a teenager. In time it would take me very far from my not-so-advantaged blue-collar beginnings.

My family all spoke our native language at home, so my first day of school was very traumatic. I was six years old, and up to that point, I had known only one language. In the classroom I felt frightened and lost. Mrs. Anderson had a great big smile and was tall, blond, blue eyed, and warm as she could be. In the beginning she called out my name, "Susana," and since I'd never responded to that name, I didn't know she was talking to me! I guess my mom forgot to tell her my most-used name was Susie. I cried most of my first day and for many days thereafter. My mom literally dragged me to school every day. I just had no clue what anyone was saying, since they all spoke English. Mrs. Anderson was very patient all the time and would take me outside, stroke my hair, and hold me tightly while I sobbed. She was as maternal as they come, making me feel safe and not different or less than any of my classmates. This went on for a few weeks, and slowly but surely, I began to understand what was being said to me and around me by the kids and the teachers. I finally understood and spoke English and began to love school, in later years never forgetting all the time Mrs. Anderson had taken with me. Later on in my life, as an adolescent, young adult, and adult, there would be many challenges, and in my mind I could always go back to this unusually kind, patient role model who didn't give up on me.

A few years after we arrived in Miami, my father convinced—and ultimately brought—each and every one of my relatives to come to Miami. Abuela Cuca became the babysitter—while Mom and Dad worked—for my sisters and me, and for my brother when he eventually came along. Cuca did this in her house after school, becoming like my second mother. I admired her spunk, style, and elegance. She had her nails and beautiful white hair done every other week, with perms to keep it tightly coiffed every couple of months. She was very creative in trying to take care of everyone yet still make ends meet. For example, I remember when she discovered from a neighbor the American way to buy—on layaway, which was a very big deal. A door-to-door salesman who spoke a little Spanish came by the neighborhood weekly to show all the housewives the beautiful home items he had in his van. And just like the other women, Cuca began to put holiday gifts, home accessories, clothes, and more on layaway. Then she applied for and got a credit card at J. Byron's, a large local department store. This was an even bigger deal—a game changer! She adorned her house with beautiful multicolored Murano glass clowns that she placed in her special curio cabinet along with other European objets d'art. Her sheets and towels were always white. Her bedspread always matched her décor. She was very sophisticated in her tastes. Unlike at our house, she had a place for everything, and everything was in its place. My mother didn't inherit that gene.

All the while, I never stopped observing what my grandmother and other family members did and how they did it, how they approached tasks and organized things—something that would definitely serve me in business later on. Cuca was also a meticulous housekeeper and a sensational cook. I'm sure my housekeeping skills have largely come from watching and assisting her. I like to say when you open the book of aphorisms to look up "a place for everything and everything in its place" that my picture is right there beside it. I've always lived that way—it's probably the Virgo in me but was definitely curated by Cuca. Cuca made it all seem like fun and not work. She washed and waxed her floors every Friday. She had a washing machine out back and hung her clothes to dry on a clothesline. She painstakingly starched and ironed my grandfather's shirts and boxer shorts. She put her heart and soul into everything she did, and it showed. And "in case" she didn't have enough to do, at some point in time—to make extra money and to help pay for her layaway and credit card bills—she began babysitting the neighbor's children. Word got out, and she then had three or four infants to babysit daily. She bought a large playpen that was placed in the middle of the living room from eight o'clock in the morning to five o'clock at night, firmly in business and earning her own money. Just like my dad, Cuca was another early entrepreneurial example to which I paid attention.

I have wonderful memories of spending as much time as I could with my maternal grandmother. She was a blessing to me. She was the queen—long before Martha Stewart—of the home-based arts of cooking, homemaking, family, welcoming friends, entertaining everyone, and the little things that make life sweet. Some may consider these things less important than others—inconsequential, even—except when you live without them. That's when you notice they're not there. That's when life isn't as rich as it can be. She was a kind, intuitive, smart, strong, humble, and compassionate woman. We were very close, and she was well versed in a variety of subjects. When she got older, we had deep conversations about forgiveness, death, and dying. In our many private conversations while she was in a nursing home, she had expressed her feelings and fear of dying. She was not just fearful of dying, she was terrified. I will be forever grateful that I was there the day she was ready to pass over to the other side.

Following my near-death experience, and just like when I asked God to help my daughter and me, that was her day to know what inexplicable calm and peace there was in what was to come. Again I prayed Psalm 23, while holding her hand. I tried to soothe her by saying there was nothing to fear and that her husband, my Abuelo Antonio, was in heaven waiting for her. She was not conscious and was hooked up to a respirator, but I knew she could hear me. As soon as I finished the prayer, I felt her soul leave her body. She was now at peace. It was no accident that I was with her to help her transition from this life to the next. I was blessed to have been the one by her side at that very instant.

Abuela Cuca was the epitome of anti-Catholic. She viewed the church as hypocritical. In Cuba she'd learned of various priests who allegedly were pedophiles, molesting boys, and nuns who were aware of what was going on. Apparently sexual abuse and exploitation were rampant, and she didn't want us exposed to any of it. Instead of siding with long-standing religious traditions about abstinence among clergy, she rebelled against them, deeming these dictums unnatural, because "God did not create human beings to be celibate," she'd say.

A year after I was born, Abuela Cuca herself had had another child—Carmen, an unexpected menopause baby. Abuela Cuca lived blocks away from Saint Mary's Cathedral and school. Ironically, my aunt Ada (Carmen's much older sister) wanted Carmen to have a Catholic upbringing and to attend school there. This was likely to the great dismay of my grandmother, though she gave in and sent her. Carmen also had First Communion. Again, I'm sure my grandmother did not endorse any of this, but those of us with Cuban blood are typically not wallflowers, and Carmen, young as she was, was no exception. Her sister, Ada, and she, as she grew, had the courage of their convictions. It would take me a while to learn to stand up for myself—even at the expense of an early, complicated marriage I was forced into, which I talk about in the next chapter. But once I took control, there was no turning back.

As far as religion was concerned, you might say work was my family's religion. As immigrants, we all had a strong, indefatigable faith in work's power to change things. My entire family was made up of incredibly industrious people—a "gene" I believe I inherited that manifested itself the moment I began working myself after school and on weekends at age fourteen (I told them I was sixteen) at Eagle Army/Navy, a small department store, so I could buy the latest fashions of the day: Madras blouses, skirts, and Bass Weejuns penny loafers. It was clear to me the whole time I was growing up that my family did whatever it could to make a living. Long, hard, often relentlessly hot and sweaty hours in Miami did nothing to deter my family from toiling to create lives as bountiful as the ones they'd left behind in a country that prior to Cuba's political blight had been almost paradise. Thanks to my parents' example, I had a powerful work ethic and never looked for the easy way around or out of things.

FLESH AND BLOOD ... AND GOOD BONES!

In Miami we essentially recreated the living arrangements we'd had in Cuba. All of our family members who emigrated lived within walking distance of one another's houses. No one could afford to buy a house, so everyone rented small homes or duplex-style apartments. We lived in northwest Miami, which was more of a blue-collar area of the city, but I didn't know any different and was generally a contented child. Dad had stashed away some money, and his dream was to own his own home. Because of his trade and mastery of construction, he would buy houses in the neighborhood. After a very intense inspection of the property, he instinctively knew if the house had "good bones." Good bones for him meant that the house had a good flow and layout—enough bedrooms and bathrooms—and that he would be able to sell it at a profit once renovated so we could move on to another house. More often than not, Dad seemed to work seven days a week. Besides working his day job, on weekends he'd gut a bathroom or knock down a wall or pull out kitchen cabinets. Mom was a trooper—never complaining—as she knew every house that Dad renovated was bigger and more beautiful than the last. She was right behind him, cleaning up the dust and debris. There was always a project in the works, and we would work side by side as I learned more and more about what Dad did and how he did it. I became a serious student of his trade. I could hand him the right tools, like someone assisting during surgery. He'd take me with him as he made the rounds to hardware stores while Mom took care of my sisters and later my baby brother. I became my dad's right-hand person—his project manager in construction vernacular—and I couldn't have been more proud of my job! It felt good to be chosen and depended upon by someone I loved and respected so much.

Though I adored my father, he was human and not without his faults. He was a perfectionist in his craft and in many ways old school, with a real Latin temperament, something that would impact my life and in fact paralyze me in unforeseen ways before I graduated from high school. What happened was an incomprehensible betrayal that would take me years to forgive and climb out of. I explore this in chapter 3.

Like most males, he loved to watch boxing matches, football, and baseball. He was also a champion dominoes player, and he rode around on an old motorcycle in his spare time—something he'd done in Cuba. He got rid of the motorcycle after it fell on top of one of my sisters while she was playing near it. Luckily she was okay. In a way he was a true Renaissance man with many eclectic interests and qualities. Among his many outstanding attributes was his love for education: he was a voracious reader. He trained his sights on the Bible, autobiographies, history, politics, health, and metaphysics, and he also loved exercise. In fact, his exercise was his work, but as long as I can remember, to make his arms hard, he always had ten- and twenty-pound dumbbells at his bedside; he pumped these daily. Though he didn't go to college, Dad educated himself for decades beyond high school and became *so* well versed in *so* many subjects, he could talk to anyone. Friends and family validated this often, as he engaged them in conversation about the most esoteric of subjects. They'd tell us how smart my father was because he knew so much about so many subjects. I'd just give them a "knowing" smile.

When my twin sisters were very young, probably the only thing Dad could never learn was their language. It was very frustrating for him not to understand the twins. They say twins develop their own vocabulary—their own form of communication—and when my sisters were young, they'd entertain themselves for hours this way. But this was no meaningless gibberish: one really knew what the other was saying. I thought it was funny, as somehow I came to understand them. But Dad did not, so once again he'd rely on me as I proudly deciphered and translated. I was fluent in "twinspeak," and Dad appreciated that. As the oldest of four children, I was his go-to child, again to help him out. Thank goodness that as my sisters got older, they all finally understood each other.

In October 2015, I was knee deep in the construction of a new house for Alan and me. Back in 2000, we'd moved into an apartment on the beach from a home in Weston—a suburb of Fort Lauderdale. We'd done that as soon as we'd become empty nesters and Lauren had gone off to college. We'd told her we wanted to be like *The Jeffersons*—move on up to the east side to the deluxe apartment in the sky—and we did! At the time we'd gone into our apartment, we had no grandchildren. Now, after fifteen years, we had twelve, and we were long overdue to give them the freedom to have a private pool and run around without any of the neighbors reporting us for being too noisy. Dad had gotten very ill while I was building our forever home, and he never had the opportunity to come to the construction site to see the house in person. I would be sure to take pictures daily to show him so that he could enjoy and be part of the construction process. It was no surprise that, like him, I had been buying, renovating, and flipping homes for the past five years. He had seen them all in person—the before and after—always beaming with pride about how he had taught me well. He was the master, and I was for sure his student.

When he passed away on February 10, 2016, at age eighty-nine, he'd been reading a book on the life of Nikola Tesla, which he kept next to his bedside with his glasses. In his last days, his children and grandchildren came to be with him during the transition. We all sat vigilantly by his hospice bed as he had long conversations with us on the prodigious number of topics about which he knew so much. We'd leave the room scratching our heads, scurrying to internet search engines to figure out what he was talking about.

Again, it was no accident that the hospice facility was ten minutes from where I live. He had congestive heart failure, end-stage COPD, and diabetes. I came over as often as I could to watch television shows with him and talk about one of his now favorite subjects—his birth country of Cuba and his youth. We also talked about metaphysical topics, my past, all the things he taught me, and how lucky I was to have him as a father. I told him I had forgiven him, let go of any anger, regret, and sadness he might have thought I'd been holding on to. I told him I now knew that everything happens for a reason and that there was nothing to forgive. He would squeeze my hand and give me one of his many loving looks as confirmation that he was happy to know, and he would mouth that he loved me. Weeks later, when he slipped into unconsciousness, and when I was alone with him, again I prayed Psalm 23. I told him it was okay to go and gave him a final goodbye kiss on his forehead. I asked Mom to come into the room, knowing he would soon be taking his last breath. Dad, I love you. Rest in peace.

We had now moved into our new house that Dad had never seen apart from the pictures I would show him on my iPad. The day he was buried, at four o'clock in the morning, our Ring Doorbell—a digital doorbell with a camera system and a cell phone app that shows you who is outside your door—mysteriously rang. Startled, I woke Alan up and ran to get my phone, immediately opening the app to see who was ringing the doorbell at that hour. Of course, there was no one physically there. I told Alan it was Dad saying, "I got to see your house. It's beautiful. I'm so proud." He was amazing—even showing up in the afterlife.

FOSTER GRANT LAND

In the event it wasn't clear at the beginning of the chapter, Dad had a kind of adventurism and wanderlust about him that could not be suppressed for long. He was a responsible, reliable, steadfast provider who never let us down, but there was another side to his personality. It's kind of like the beach ball on which you try to sit in the swimming pool. You can keep it down for only so long until it sky-rockets, full force, up through the surface—moonward, in fact. Dad had gone from Cuba to New York and Cuba to Miami. Now it was time for our family's manifest destiny all the way to California. Had it been the 1800s, I'm certain Dad would have had us on a wagon train headed straight for gold rush territory. Fortunately, there were now automobiles, and we packed our car to the gills, setting out for what we'd heard was another paradise.

Some of my mom's cousins, Ricardo and Sonny, had moved out west some years earlier. It was 1963, Florida's construction industry was slowing down, and the cousins encouraged my dad to pull up stakes and move on out. My brother, Peter, had been born two years earlier, and the six of us piled into our powder-blue and white 1959 Buick station wagon. It was the end of the Miami story and the beginning of the Los Angeles one. Mom sat in the back seat with the twins, and Peter was on her lap. At barely thirteen years old, I got to sit in the front passenger seat to read the maps and navigate. Dad really trusted me, and this was one more example.

BRAND NEW START

When we arrived in California, we had lunch with the cousins, Dad rented a furnished apartment that they'd lined up for us, we unpacked whatever we'd brought that had fit in the car—and just like that, we were home. Dad quickly found construction work, just as the cousins had said he would. The apartment he rented was on Rampart Street in West Los Angeles—a community filled with immigrants, a melting pot from all over the world. Up until then, I had never been exposed to so much diversity. Just like ours, the apartments around us were filled with different cultures, languages, skin tones, and fragrant cooking smells that wafted from their open kitchen windows. Apartment living was really foreign to us, as we had always lived in a house. This was a more communal experience, with people always walking around, sitting on the catwalk outside their apartments, or walking their dogs. It was mayhem. I don't think Dad ever got used to the constant noise.

After matriculating in the local junior high school, I was super excited. It was a new adventure. Unlike stifling Miami, LA was surrounded by beautiful mountains and cool weather in the morning and at night. I couldn't wait to go to school to make new friends in my new city. I'd always walked to school in Miami, but this would not be possible in LA. On the first day of school, Mom walked me to the bus stop on Wilshire Boulevard—as I recall, a long seven-block walk. Luckily there were other kids waiting for the public bus as well. She told me to put in my dime to pay for my fare and get off when the other kids did. She said, "I won't be walking you to the bus stop every day, so please remember to learn the route, as you will be taking it every day from home to school and back home." The bus stopped at King Junior High—my first day in ninth grade.

The extent of my school's diversity in Miami involved Caucasians, African Americans, and a few Cubans (the rest would come with a continuously evolving Cuban political climate as I entered high school). But California was the land of diversity—a different world entirely. My classes were brimming with Asian kids, Mexican kids, Middle Eastern kids, European kids, and many other ethnicities and religions to which I had never been exposed. I made great friends from different cultures, which really stretched my traditional Cuban horizons.

On weekends my cousins took us to Disneyland, Knott's Berry Farm, the Griffith Observatory, and all the Southern California hot spots—"exotic" places I'd only read about or seen in movies and could not have imagined ever visiting from my corner of the world. We'd spend hours in places like Redondo Beach or watching surfers in Laguna—it was an aspirational kind of "California Dreamin" life, except that I never felt quite at home there. And I guess somehow the universe understood that.

On a not-so-typical morning about a year after we'd arrived, we awoke to a bona fide California earthquake. Statistics show that most of these occur around dawn, and this one was no exception. My dad was thrown from his bed, ending up flat on the floor, frightened out of his mind. As much as he'd read in the realm of continuously educating and improving himself, somehow he'd been absent from the school of earthquake edification. He didn't understand how something like that could happen. With the tropical storms and hurricanes, phenomena my family had experienced many times, generally there was time to prepare. But an earthquake was another story.

"That's it. We're heading back to Miami," he told my mother a few days later, unwilling to go through another quake. The Buick in which we'd driven out there had seen better days and no way could have made the three-thousand-mile trek back, so Dad sold the car. We packed up our belongings and boarded a train, which snaked through the blazing, ruggedly beautiful Southwest on its way to Florida. In less than a week, we were home—finally back home.

In California I'd been quite smitten with a typing class and its wonderful teacher. Somehow it came easily to me, and back in school in Miami, I quickly advanced to Typing II. I also took regular high school classes such as algebra and advanced math, English, and geography—the latter always held my attention, so reading Dad's maps along the way to California had been easy and fun. I put a lot of energy into classes in business, business management, business law, business writing, résumé writing, and more—all part of the new vocational education program. Vocational office education prepared students for a trade or a craft. I wanted in and told my parents there were very few slots available to be filled and that I was going to apply. The program was conditional, however: not just anyone could decide to take it and do so. You had to be selected, excel, and remain worthy of it. There was no coasting. From these classes I acquired all sorts of business and office skills that would not only serve me well in my professional future; they'd be my ticket out of an increasingly suffocating first marriage.

CHAPTER 3

A TWIST OF FATE

Focus on what you are moving toward rather
than what you are leaving behind.

ALAN COHEN

When I was in high school, back in Miami from LA, Cubans began pouring in to Florida's east coast where I lived. Prior to that, the typical track had taken them to Florida's Gulf Coast—places like Ybor City, where they'd find work in the region's flourishing cigar industry. There was a sprinkling, if that, of Cubans in my classes until high school, and I certainly didn't speak Spanish to anybody except my family. In fact, most people didn't realize I was Cuban. But in the mid-1960s, it was as if the door to Miami swung wide open, and there they were: a major influx of Cuban immigrants. I'd open my locker, and by the time I closed it, someone would be behind me speaking Spanish. They'd identify me as "one of them" and approach me in the lunchroom, study hall, and outside on the grounds of the school. And I didn't like it.

My parents had been naturalized, and by law, as their child, it had extended to me. As a teenager, I was almost ashamed to associate with these immigrants. I wanted nothing to do with them. I wanted to be identified as the American I was.

"We don't understand. Don't you speak any Spanish?" my Cuban classmates would demand in Spanish when I'd respond in a stilted way to whatever they'd asked me. Every question and conversation was in Spanish. They would continue to talk to me in Spanish, and I just didn't want any part of it. Even in California, which had been more of a cultural melting pot, somehow I'd gotten the message that to be cool, one had to be American, and that's how I identified myself in school.

When I went home after school, I could not escape my heritage. The Cuban tradition is to celebrate life with high-spirited parties every weekend at the home of a relative. We'd play salsa music and loved to listen to Tito Puente, Benny Moré, Celia Cruz, Olga Guillot (my mother's favorite singer), and so many others. We'd dance and cook, cook, cook! The food was fragrant, spicy, and abundant—falling off the tables, which could hardly contain it all. The food and festivities were exemplary of the warm, effusive culture from which I'd come—whether I embraced it publicly or not. There were also rounds, always chaperoned, of coming-of-age parties with as much revelry as weddings and replete with bands and singers (the way Gloria Estefan got her start—I actually met her fronting a band at these parties!). These events would celebrate Cuban girls turning fifteen and sixteen, and one of the gatherings would alter the course of my life.

In Cuba—and "Miami, Cuba" as it was—like my mother's generation, girls not married by age eighteen were considered old maids. While the conversation never contained any specifics about that at my house, my mother had married at nineteen, and it was basically understood that this was the goal. I had Cuban high school acquaintances and friends (yes, I did become friendly with Spanish-speaking girls after a time) who spent their senior year planning their engagements and weddings. For Americans it was all about getting into college, which was all I ever wanted, but my culture would pull me away from this.

At one particular "Sweet 15" party, I was introduced to Orlando. Just four years my senior, he was far more traditional. He'd not embraced life as it was or could be in America. Orlando worked construction as a day laborer. His parents, who spoke no English, worked in factories. He had never gone to college and had absolutely no interest in it. Maybe it was my culture and what was going on all around me with my friends and their marriage talk, but I began to feel as though he were my boyfriend—like I was *supposed* to feel that way. I definitely felt peer pressure from the other girls, many of whom were wearing engagement rings and had summer weddings scheduled just a few weeks or even just days after high school graduation. I was very conflicted about the appropriate thing to do.

Orlando and I had been dating for about six months when out of the blue my father took me aside one day, asking if he had "touched me." Again, in the Cuban culture, there weren't many examples of young people having the proverbial birds-and-bees talk with their parents, and I'd certainly never had it, but I knew enough to remain a virgin, and that's exactly what I was. On the other hand, I'd always had a close relationship with my father, so I believed the right thing to do (and I thought I was safe enough) was to answer that yes, he had "touched me" but that we had not actually had sex. My father turned five different shades of purple.

"That's it!" he exclaimed. "After graduation, you're getting married. I am *not* going to have my family disrespected—or have a daughter who is *not* a virgin when she gets married."

Married? To Orlando? But I was a virgin! I'd done nothing to disgrace myself or my family. Dad and Mom knew marriage was not what I had in mind and that I had been planning to go to college—certainly not to marry Orlando! I remember standing there in utter shock—as though someone had put a pillow over my head, suffocating me, letting the air out of my life—repeating to my father over and over that I was a virgin and was going to remain a virgin. I'd not allowed Orlando to take that from me. Marriage was not what I had in mind. At that point, I saw marriage to Orlando as a dead end. He was only my second boyfriend, the first having been a crush when I was fourteen. I certainly liked Orlando, but … love? Marriage? My culture aside, what does anyone know about that at eighteen? It was not the path to the kind of life I'd envisioned for myself.

The summer between my junior and senior years, because of our excellent office skills, two classmates and I had been chosen for an internship at Eastern Airlines. This entailed dressing up in business suits each day, including very grown-up stockings and heels, and taking two buses each way for the hour-long trip to the airline offices and back. As an intern, I spent the summer getting coffee but also taking dictation, typing, and filing—applying the business skills I'd been learning and practicing in my high school classes to the protocols and procedures of a real business. I couldn't get enough! The exposure was almost euphoric for me, and I knew I wanted to go to college and be a viable member of the professional world. I wanted to get into management, and with a degree in hand, an office job would be a stepping-stone. My internship would open doors. Now my father was trampling my dreams and goals—snuffing them out—just like that. I was devastated. My life would change forever and clearly not for the best. I wasn't in love with Orlando, and even if I were, marrying so soon was not a part of my plan.

When you come from a traditional culture with an old-school family, and certainly as a young female in the 1960s, there is no way out. At least I hadn't figured it out yet. It wasn't as though I could leave my house and have somewhere to go. Relatives would not have sided with me. At one point before the marriage, my need to escape my terrible fate became so all-consuming that I began sleepwalking, as though trying to run away—unlocking the front door and slipping out into the night—whereupon my father would go and claim me from the street. In my waking hours I had even thought about living under an overpass—on my own—*anything* was going to be better than the way I was now destined to spend the rest of my life. I was desperate. Though I'd worked since the age of fourteen on weekends and after school until nine o'clock at night to be able to buy my own clothes and other things a teenage girl might want, at that point I had no job. I had no money. I had no power. I was completely impotent in any kind of decision made about me.

I reluctantly confronted my fate, trying to face it head on. I had long talks with Orlando, making it clear that when we married, I wanted to go to college. He always replied, "Yes. Sure. No problem. Of course." But once we were married, it wasn't to happen.

Our wedding pictures in June of 1968 tell the story of what was in my heart and soul, which were empty. The words *diminished* and *defeated* don't begin to describe how I felt that day. My father, whom I loved and adored, and who had loved and trusted me all those years we'd worked as a team on his many projects, had betrayed me. In a strange way, when that realization took hold, I began to look at the dark marriage I was facing as at least a way out of the house of the one who'd done this to me.

SOLITARY CONFINEMENT

I was absent in that marriage. I was fighting hard not to fade away. I'm sure I had only a few of what today would be called emotional tools, but my husband had absolutely none. Just like his parents, he clearly didn't know how to communicate. He was an only child, and I would come to learn at occasional Sunday dinners at my in-law's that no one actually spoke in his house. Orlando was a Jekyll-and-Hyde kind of personality; coming home from work, if something irked him—either something from his day or something I'd done or not done in the house—he wouldn't talk to me for days on end. Sometimes his sulking would last two weeks. All too often I felt as though, for reasons unknown to me, he was punishing me, and it wasn't up for discussion. Living that way is very painful. I would cry myself to sleep, and he couldn't have cared less.

I was going mad. My days and nights consisted of housework, television, cooking, laundry, more housework, anticipating the little or no appreciation or communication coming from my spouse, and a sadness that metastasized more and more with each passing week. Orlando would come home from work, flop down in a chair, and expect dinner. His clothes had to be washed, and everything had to be done perfectly, no matter what kind of day I'd had. That's the way his mother had raised him. He was an obnoxious, overbearing, uncommunicative mama's boy.

LIFE WITHOUT LIMITS

In chapter one I talked about receiving a life review during my near-death experience in the trunk. This is like a movie of one's entire life. Though this information may be hard to imagine, during my life review I came to understand that the course of events in our lives happens the way it does so we can complete our soul contract. Our soul contract is something for which we sign on, in a manner of speaking, to learn the lessons we're supposed to learn in this lifetime.

We decide on and make an agreement before we are born about the kind of physical life we're going to have on earth—everything we're going to experience. Hard as it was for me to understand and to accept, the kidnapping was something for which I'd signed on. Each of us decides what our lives will look like—or even whether we will come back in the physical body at all. In fact, many souls who come back in physical form have agreed to take on immeasurable suffering: homelessness, murder, terminal illness, excruciating loss, imprisonment, starvation, torture—all so they can learn for themselves and the people around them can learn the lessons they in turn are supposed to learn from the experiences of these other souls.

There is always a dark and treacherous path to the light, and the connection between people in getting to the light is indescribable—limitless. There is light beneath any darkness—light that cannot be extinguished.

I would learn that because everything I went through is a life script (soul contract) I'd written for myself, there was "no one other than myself" to forgive. I walked around feeling angry and resentful and hurt and everything else for years, but once I found out that I'd signed up for this experience, I needed to forgive myself—not keep blaming my "perpetrators." It's not an easy concept, and it takes thought and work, but once it becomes clear, life becomes a very different experience.

I needed to forgive myself for the way I felt about my father, about Orlando, and forgive myself for feeling like a victim for so many years. Sometimes I think the people in our lives—and certainly in mine—put on an Academy Award performance in whatever they do—unwitting or otherwise—so that the lessons we need to learn will be so apparent we cannot miss them. And for that we actually need to be grateful—I know I do.

So again, eventually I would come to understand that my time in an unbearable marriage was part of what I'd signed on for. It would take courage to find out, which I talk about later, but I'd benefit from having had the experience.

From day one, and because I clearly knew none of this for a long time after that marriage ended, the only thing that kept me going was the birth of my daughter Gina in August of 1969. I keep saying that it's painful going into what should be a sacred relationship when you know from the beginning it is not where you belong—and staying in it. But it produced Gina, who lifted my heart. Her tiny but profound presence would inspire me to figure it out.

When she was about a year and a half old, I awoke one morning with a plan—a wild idea—certainly unconventional for that era and especially for the culture from which I'd come. When my husband left for work, I called my mother-in-law and confided in her that the marriage was in trouble. As expected, I hadn't gotten a lot of support from my mom or my dad, both of whom had decided that when the baby was born, that would be the answer for me. That was what I needed. That was *all* I needed. Not so! Though I loved Gina with all my heart, I wanted to be both a mother and businessperson. My mother-in-law was eyeing retirement and loved to babysit Gina. I told her I needed to get out of the house and go to a job every day. Though I didn't believe the following myself, I had to tell her something and said I thought this would strengthen the marriage. Orlando was her only child, and I was certain she'd do anything to ensure his happiness. I was giving her an opportunity to save his marriage. She agreed to talk to him, tell him what was necessary here, and the next thing I knew, I was able to look for a job.

With my well-honed office skills, experience at Eastern Airlines, and letters of recommendation from my vocational teachers, I had no problem getting one. I went to work as a secretary for two wonderful men, Ira Cohen and David Blumberg, in a commercial real estate office. They bought and sold office buildings, shopping centers, and warehouses, and they managed the properties. It was my first exposure to real estate, which would serve me a couple of years down the road when I'd land what would turn out to be an increasingly defining job for me.

But first, it's almost funny to say now (though it was not back then) that the only car between Orlando and me was a fiery red Pontiac GTO—stick shift and all. He agreed to let me use it, except for the fact that I had no idea how to drive a stick. A good lesson based on a saying I once heard: *You can't ride the clutch and mash the gas at the same time.* While this appeared to be a literal lesson so I could get to work and back, years later, in the aftermath of the kidnapping, it would serve as a metaphor in a time of unfathomable breakdown and crisis. I'd learn that I'd been dismantled, and I would have to learn, as I show in chapters 6 and 7, how to put myself back together.

For the moment, I learned about the car, but that didn't mean I was comfortable. It had a noisy muffler and sounded like the muscle car it was—like the one they drive in *The Fast and Furious* movie franchise. I was mortified driving to and from work because everyone could hear me coming. But that was actually a small price to pay for a measure of independence. I was self-supporting and could open my own checking account. My bosses valued and supported me, and it all fed my soul. I'd finally reclaimed a little freedom, though no matter how challenging my day, and even if I got home a little late, Orlando would expect dinner on the table and a clean house. Perhaps he wasn't unlike a lot of men of his day, but in a marriage that had begun the way it had, everything was amplified.

We'd been living in a duplex apartment since we married. Orlando's parents decided it might work well for all of us if they bought a house and we all moved in together. That way, my mother-in-law would always be there for Gina, and they could sleep a little later without our worrying about schedules, dropping her off and picking her up, or anything else. The house they'd selected had ample bedrooms, beautiful terrazzo floors, and a big backyard for Gina. I wasn't sure what I thought about the idea but went along with it because I was basically numb. I'd gained some independence, respect, and validation from the owners of my company for my daily contribution to the business, but at the end of the day, I always had to go home.

At dinner in the new place, after a nominal greeting, again no one ever spoke. No one ever asked what anyone did at work that day or what else was going on. Dinners were cold, dark, and silent. Afterward, Orlando and his father plopped down in their easy chairs to watch TV, saying nothing to anybody. I rushed through my meals to take Gina outside and sit with her on the swing or run around in the grass until bedtime. The Helen Reddy song "You and Me Against the World" wouldn't come along for a few more years (and I'd find myself singing it to Gina when it did), but the feelings were already there, deep inside, until the day they just had to come out.

PRISON BREAK

After six months at my job, I decided couldn't face one more night raising my child in that dysfunctional, joyless environment. The 119th Street route I'd take to work and back from the new house skirted Miami Dade College, and each time I saw it, though it made me feel frustrated and angry that I was trapped, something inside me lit up. The buildings were billboards to the future—neon signs screaming "College! College! College!" and they called to me.

The thing is, what I did wasn't exactly planned. The pain, depression, panic, and desperation of the past couple of years welled up inside of me, and the dam burst. The prison doors swung wide open—by my own hand. I packed my belongings, picked up my child, and walked out, proclaiming as loudly as I could, *"I'm not doing this anymore!"* I felt emboldened to take charge of my life. It was as if someone or something had taken over my mind and body, and there I went.

But the ride to my parents' house was fraught with anxiety. I cried the whole way there, tail between my legs. Here I was, about to throw myself at their mercy—throw myself at the man who'd betrayed his daughter and the woman who'd supported him. I hoped against hope that they would find a way to understand me and accept their granddaughter and me into their home. No one in my family had ever gotten divorced, and I knew they thought it was shameful that I wasn't working things out with my husband and had been so unhappy for so long. And now it was over—really, really over. But no matter what I had to do, I was not going back.

When I arrived, sobbing, clutching my child, they could tell I was exhausted. I was disconnected—more like a shell than a human being. Something must have turned over in them, because they knew they had no alternative but to let us stay with them.

Gina and I moved into a spare bedroom, and Orlando kept coming over to visit his daughter, begging me to come home. But that place where he lived, where I'd barely survived, was no home. I dutifully went to dinner with him a time or two, as he was persistent, but it was pointless, and I stopped because I didn't want to mislead him. I didn't want to be unfair and make him think I would consider returning. I was not now or ever going back.

At age twenty-one I filed for divorce, starting over, saving up enough money to purchase a car, as I no longer had Orlando's, and working toward eventually getting a little apartment for Gina and me.

A job at GAC Corporation, a large land development entity, followed. It paid more money, and I needed all I could get. The company's Miami headquarters was in an eleven-story building where thousands of people worked. Many if not most of the properties on Florida's west coast were developed by GAC Corporation. I was hired to work as administrative assistant to John Khouri, head of the international division, which focused on land sales to German nationals.

A few months into the job, I happened to see a company posting for an executive assistant in the office of the president—high up on the top floor. I applied, knowing it paid better, though I'd been doing so well in my current job that they said they didn't want me to go. But I was a single mother with a daughter to support. Every time

I got a new job was a bump up for me. In the president's office, I thought I'd died and gone to heaven. There was plush carpeting and people constantly circulating with carts and little trays featuring fresh croissants and coffee. The environment was something like the TV series *Mad Men*. The air in the conference room during meetings turned blue—like a barroom. The smoke was so thick you had difficulty finding the person next to you.

We had lunch served to us every day rather than having to go down to the cafeteria or rush across the street to Junior's for split pea soup as I had in my previous position. The additional money I was earning—though most of it was going toward supporting my child and paying my parents something toward Gina and my rent and food and, of course, my savings—could also go toward a more stylish wardrobe. I was never foolish and irresponsible that way, but in working with the president, it was important to look the part. What's more, I felt confident, competent, and totally appreciated every day, and I was not going home to a hellish environment with Orlando. I was actually making more money at that point than my father, though out of respect for him, I'd never have told him.

This brings me to think about a quote from Chaucer that I read quite a long time ago but still find so appropriate: "There is an end to everything, to good things as well."

I'd been in the president's office three or four months when a folder about cutbacks crossed my desk. I remember the feeling in the pit of my stomach. There were half a dozen women like me working in the office of the president in addition to a bevy of male assistants, and the truth is that because of the crowd, there wasn't as much for me to do as there'd been in other jobs. I loved every day but frankly felt less challenged, which was going to help in the decision I was about to make. Other key executives had their assistants as well, and

I instantly knew that if the company was cutting back, as the last hired/low man on the totem pole, I'd be the first to go. My search was on for the next rung.

Sipping my cup of coffee a few days later, I opened the Sunday *Miami Herald*. An ad for an executive assistant to the president of an unnamed company stood out to me with a telephone number to call. It said to ask for Norman Silber. The next day during lunch at GAC, I went to a phone on another floor and called.

Walking into the lobby for my interview, I was dizzy from the beehive of activity at this new company. What I didn't know at the time (and apparently neither did prospective clients and others who went in for meetings) was that the impressive lobby, well-coiffed receptionist, and long, meandering walk through warrens of desks were the accoutrements of Midwest Mortgage, which was leasing space in the back to IRE Group (Alan Levan, my soon-to-be boss at IRE, had been connected with the owner of Midwest at one time). It was a fabulous facade—I was duly impressed, which I'm quite sure was their goal for everyone. For a business that consisted of three employees, including myself when I was hired and a fourth that came on board soon afterward, operating in about five hundred square feet—the size of a two-car garage—this was a pretty good situation.

My interview involved typing and shorthand tests, something I could have done in my sleep. Norman was very thorough, and I got the feeling he liked petite brunettes. I just happened to look like Cher, my waist-length black hair parted straight down the middle. Sure, I knew my stuff, but I was also early 1970s hip and chic—which wasn't lost on Norman!

As the business's attorney and administrator, Norman offered me a lot of money plus overtime. Facade or not, I knew I'd come to the right place.

"I'm a single mother," I told him. "I also need insurance." I was given everything I needed and more, and Gina and I were able to find a nice garden apartment in Dadeland, an up-and-coming young neighborhood in South Miami. In time, IRE moved to a beautiful office of its own in downtown Coral Gables. The office was walking distance from Gina's preschool and elementary school, and with the afterschool care until 6:00 p.m. I was able to afford, it almost seemed that the torturous time I'd spent living with Orlando had not been for nothing. Using it as a frame of reference, occasionally I'd think back to just how far I'd come, and rarely a day passed when I was not *grateful for every single thing*: big or small. I was building a good life for my daughter and me, and I was in control. Figuring my way out of a marriage and a life where I wasn't valued and into a life of self-reliance and self-respect where I was, was a kind of spiritual caffeine. I felt it in my head, my heart, and down deep in my soul.

I RISE

By the time IRE moved to Coral Gables, the company had grown and expanded to include hundreds of employees. We could have filled nearly every desk at the labyrinth Midwest Mortgage, the building where the company had started, just by way of comparison. IRE was focused on real estate limited partnerships and was beyond successful. As we grew, in addition to working with Norman and doing things for Alan such as managing his calendar, I was given more and more responsibility. This was in the realm of managing the twenty-plus-member administration department, letters to broker-dealers, and all of the company's printing and mailing brochures, marketing brochures, and other back-office responsibilities. Work went on day and night, sometimes weekends as well, and I got to bring Gina, who was six months older than Alan's older son, Donny. As toddlers, they'd play together on the carpet as their parents set about conquering the world!

What's more, Norman and Alan insisted I enroll in anything I thought would improve my performance at IRE—fully paid. They left it up to me, and this included courses at Dale Carnegie; Toastmasters, where my abject terror about speaking before people soon melted into awards for doing so (this would help a lot during various department meetings, some of which I led); business classes at the University of Miami; and more. I studied hard no matter what I was trying to learn or do and won various awards for excellence. I was determined to succeed. I also got the opportunity to get a Series 7 license, which would mean I was authorized to work as a general securities representative. This included sales of corporate securities, municipal securities, investment company securities, variable annuities, direct participation programs, options, and government securities. It would make me more of an asset to IRE.

When the bottom fell out of the economy in 1974, IRE had to change course and start managing the properties it had acquired. Quite prudently, and using what I and many others (even those not so close to him!) have always called his visionary prowess, Alan shut down all real estate buying—all vast expenditures of that nature. This meant the broker-dealers who'd brought IRE new investors were basically stopped in their tracks. They would no longer be paid commissions. Alan made a whole lot of enemies, because he'd made a whole lot of people a whole lot of money and was continuing to until he pulled the plug. But he'd seen the future. Things just could not continue the way they were in a struggling and very soon stalled economy, and in the ensuing months, those companies like IRE that did not pull the purchasing plug went under. We went on by tightening our belts and redirecting our focus. In the future, IRE would begin buying real estate again and diversifying into much more, but for four years we did what Alan knew we had to do to survive.

In the late 1970s I met Mitchell, an attorney with offices in our building, who kept coming to our office as he was doing some work for IRE. We started going to dinner, and I could see he was a kind man. I felt Gina and I needed some stability, as we'd been on our own for about eight years. Mitchell clearly had the financial stability gene, and we married.

A FAMILIAR FAITH

It wasn't because I'd been surrounded by Jewish bosses and coworkers everywhere, or the fact that Mitchell was Jewish, that I converted, as my religion was never a consideration for my fiancé. But it mattered more to his family, and I wanted to do it to make life easier for everyone. Paramount to that, I was powerfully drawn to Judaism in the first place in ways I could not describe. In the few ways I could, Judaism was like a second skin to me. It was familiar, and it was home.

I sought out one of the neighborhood rabbis, Rabbi Edwin Farber, who had a very small, conservative synagogue. We were about the same age, and I was instantly comfortable with him. In the Jewish religion, when someone expresses the desire to convert, it's traditional for the rabbi to try to discourage him or her, as it is imperative that such a radical change in beliefs, adherences, and practices be a commitment of the highest order. There was absolutely no hesitation on my part—in fact, I had a profound knowing that this was my path, and I couldn't wait to get to the finish line. Many years later, I would meet a rabbi who was very psychic and fully immersed in the

Kabballah who greeted me with the words that he'd been "waiting for me"—that through his meditation he'd learned I'd been a rabbi in Spain during the Inquisition and in fact had lines identical to a Star of David etched into my hand. *What?* While I was drawn to Jewish mysticism, this was something way out for me—until he lifted my palm and showed me.

"You were ordered to renounce your faith or be forced out of your country, imprisoned, or lose your life," he explained, "and by carving the Star of David, you remained indelibly connected to Judaism." My paternal Abuela had immigrated to Cuba from the Canary Islands, an archipelago of Spain sixty-two miles west of Morocco, so there was definitely some kind of family reference to Spain that likely went back generations.

Rabbi Farber and I met twice a week over about a six-month period. I had to read a lot of prescribed material, both books and scripture, and I started picking up books on my own. Among these was information on Jewish meditation, the Zohar, and the Kabbalah. Though it was long before the kidnapping, I felt some kind of mystical pull toward many of these books, though I could not put it into words. As for the traditional material, late in the process, two different rabbis tested me on what I had learned, and in a word, I aced it—all of it. It had been effortless. I passed with flying colors. As I said, second skin.

In the conversion process, I was taken to a mikveh—the traditional ritual bath where you purify yourself for the life you have chosen. This took place in a tiled underground room where I fully immersed myself into "living water," or water from springs or groundwater wells. There was also a second one where both my daughter and I were purified in a lake. Both mikveh ceremonies were beautiful, and I will never forget them.

My parents were simply happy that I'd finally found happiness with a partner and that I'd have some companionship and Gina would finally have a father. I wanted a father who was really present in her life for her, which Orlando was not.

Mitchell—who'd not been married prior to meeting me and had always wanted a child—and I were soon blessed with two. We already had Gina, and then Lauren came along in 1981—born to me long after a time when I'd been told I'd not be able to have more children. This was something Mitchell had generously accepted when we married, so Lauren's birth was an indescribably happy event.

At twenty-two, a couple of years out of the insanity with Orlando, there was no denying the existence of a mind-body connection. I was still recovering from it. I was exhausted. The stress of going through a divorce—any divorce—doesn't help no matter how bad the relationship was, though I'd certainly been carving out the kind of life I'd deserved. I'd been in considerable pain and was told I had a baseball-sized tumor on my ovary. A painful surgery to remove both the tumor and the ovary followed, and fortunately it was not cancer. But in fact, for some reason the doctor had asked me if, while he was going in, I wanted him to do a hysterectomy! Of course I said no—unless it was cancer and he believed he needed to remove everything else. I was only twenty-two! Nevertheless, given the extent of the surgery, the results prompted the doctor to tell me I'd never have to worry about using birth control again. I used none, and in time, because the universe apparently had other plans for me, Lauren was born. I loved her with all my being, and as I said in chapter one, I'm certain that among the many reasons she'd been born was to give me a reason not to give up in that trunk. As I protected her, she protected me.

EVERYTHING'S FINE UNTIL IT'S NOT

When Lauren was about four months old, I was in the process of returning to work at IRE, still (and always) committed to working long hours. I decided the thing to do was to find a live-in house-keeper/nanny. I hired Petrona: the quintessential sweet, kind, gentle, fiftyish Salvadoran grandmother who would remain with our family for twenty-five years—long after Lauren was grown and out of the house—and who would end up surviving the kidnapping with us when Lauren was seven.

Mitchell tried to be a good father to Gina, now going through her prickly teenage years, so there were challenges there, and of course he doted on Lauren. Sometimes I think the rocky relationship between Gina and Mitchell may have had some bearing on my decision to end our seven-year marriage, as a mother's instincts are to protect and nurture her children. But the other side of it was that we simply grew apart physically and emotionally. I worked long hours, much longer than he did, which can cause imbalance if people don't make resolving the rift it creates a priority. We didn't.

I have to say that a second divorce was embarrassing. Granted, divorce was much more common and acceptable in the 1980s than it had been the first time I'd initiated it—a young single mother with my old-school culture trying to suck me back in and keep me beaten down. There were a thousand reasons I'd had for the first divorce, but with Mitchell I'd been older. We were two successful adults who'd chosen one another. Yet it had just become wrong for us. When I finally "met" the right one, I would discover he'd been inches away from me on the other side of the desk for fifteen years.

CHAPTER 4

ALAN IN THIS LIFETIME

Souls tend to go back to who feels like home.

N. R. HEART

Working with Alan was one thing; marrying him was another.

In 1972, when Norman Silber hired me to work at IRE, it never occurred to me that anything like marriage would happen. I was raising a toddler, just out of a marriage that should never have been, and Alan had been married just a few years and had his first child as well. We grew to respect and appreciate one another as employee and employer, and in time I went through a second marriage, but anything more than life at the office was not a consideration. Then again, destiny is destiny.

I have strong ideas about destiny. After my near-death experience, the struggling, studying, and working I'd done to make sense of it and the opening of my body, mind, heart, and soul to allow everything to manifest, I'd come to the conclusion that so often we are with the same people in past and present lives, circling each other from life to life. We may have a different relationship with the same people, but they are with us. Do you ever feel that your "bossy" cousin is more like a mother, or that since you were twelve years old you've been so comfortable with your best friend's "pesky" brother (pesky to her, but not to you) that it's almost like you are an old married couple? Perhaps you were together in that way at one time.

During my near-death experience, I was told that we choose our life's path before we are born: we decide to whom we'll be born, the obstacles we'll face throughout our lives, and the choices we'll make. That's the life script I talk about. Alan and I were fated to meet, work together, and ultimately make the relationship more intimate and permanent no matter what. But the not knowing part is what makes living in the present as surprising as it is. It makes life new, exciting, challenging, and rich.

It's true we have no control over the economy (well, okay, that's debatable, so let's say we have no control over it in a spiritual sense!). When I saw that layoffs were imminent at GAC Corporation and felt certain I'd be among the first to go, a timely ad in the Sunday *Miami Herald* led me to my future in the most comprehensive way (please see chapter 3). I found myself in the right place at the right time, with Norman and Alan giving me more and more responsibility and opportunity as the company grew from electric typewriters to the early days of rudimentary computers—the ones where the paper had perforated edges—and beyond; from just three ambitious people to a few hundred highly motivated employees.

Motivation is also important in a marriage. And perhaps it's a cliché that marriage is sacred, as many people don't tend to treat it as such, but I surely believe it. Marriage is about the most courageous act two people can undertake, and sometimes it takes an act of God to see it through. That said, working with someone—even for fifteen years—and then marrying the person is like finding yourselves in a place where you've substituted one language with another. You were fluent together in French, and now Spanish is what's spoken at home. Okay, maybe not Spanish, as it would be too easy for me, so let's say Greek. What's more, I'd achieved executive status at IRE (now the holding company for Atlantic Federal, renamed BankAtlantic), and when we married, transitioning each morning from our lives at home to those we'd always had at the office and then back again at night took some work, at least on my part. The dynamic was different. But I hadn't considered that going in. Alan, on the other hand, is the same even-tempered human being under any circumstances, so I may have struggled a lot more than he did.

Somehow at home, I thought it was okay for the white gloves to come completely off. It never is. I'd had one unhappy and one mediocre marriage, so it may be fair to say I didn't know a lot about how to be married. Alan had been married right out of college and for many years at the point he and Terri separated and ultimately divorced, but somehow, despite the turmoil he'd experienced, he knew more than I did about how to conduct oneself in a relationship. While being honest and relaxed with one another is how it should be, letting it all hang out without giving much thought to what one says and does really isn't. I was guilty of that kind of thing, to the point of sulking, yelling, and slamming doors instead of communicating as an adult. As different as I thought I was from Orlando, some of his behavior—a huge catalyst in why I ran from that marriage—was clearly evident in me. I couldn't believe it! Maybe I took liberties with Alan because I felt we were so familiar with one another that it would be all right. It certainly was not. Alan and I had had a highly supportive and productive working relationship for a very long time, and he surely must have wondered just who he married.

When he'd needed to begin focusing on BankAtlantic, traveling all the time from Coral Gables to Fort Lauderdale, where BankAtlantic's executive offices were, he was away from IRE and would constantly call me for information and advice.

"What about this? What about that? Why are we doing this? Why have we gotten that?" I was a close and trusted advisor, intimately involved in all things business. You might say we were office soul mates. So why couldn't I manage myself in a marriage to the very same wonderful man?

COURTING ANSWERS

Over lunches, most of what we discussed was business, because that had been the only way we'd interacted for years. It was pretty much all we knew how to talk about together, and it seemed safe and familiar, though as time went on, there was clearly something more for us. There were feelings we were unable to articulate. But along with business, we also shared a penchant for motivational movers and shakers like Tom Peters, Harold Geneen, Jack Welch, and Stephen Covey, something else we could be comfortable talking about. I was a voracious reader of business and motivational books, and I'd suggest we buy a book or two, to which Alan would agree. In lieu of artwork, I made sure to hang Stephen Covey posters with maxims and affirmations all over the office so the staff would benefit as well. Alan and I would talk about what we'd read (or he'd be so busy, he'd ask me to summarize the books) and what we saw each day as we passed the posters on the walls. They were always good topics to share, something powerful we had in common, because both of us were open to growth and change. We encouraged and validated one another. But when we decided to tie the knot, though I loved him more than anything, I didn't know how to apply the same principles and ideals to a marriage. We'd essentially known one another most of our adult lives (I was twenty-two when I started at IRE). We'd celebrated business and personal victories and had supported one another through dark times. We were certainly friends. We shared a bond going in that so many couples never have. So, what was it that I didn't know?

What I did know was that I am more upfront with people in my dealings with them and my communication style. I get to the point. Alan is a great leader, and his presentation is different. He has a slow, studied, almost tacit kind of eloquence in the way he communicates. He clearly makes his point but takes a different road to get there. I also have Latin blood, which makes me somewhat fiery and sometimes makes us polar opposites. But whether that had any bearing on things or not, we needed to find a way to make it all work. We had our new life together, and we also had to establish some cohesion for our combined families. Though nothing is perfect, there had to be a sense of ease, comfort, laughter, and joy in our home, not ongoing tension and a living room war. The fact is, it would take us years to learn how to effectively communicate, but we were determined to do it.

GOOD AND WELFARE ... AND THE SALSA KING

In our business life together, we attended many seminars. One in particular was a seminar on a concept called "Good and Welfare." The idea was that if you had a problem with an employee, you'd write it down instead of immediately barking in a kind of knee-jerk reaction. Over time, you might fill a legal pad full of items, big and small, which meant it was time to call a meeting with that individual. It was a very civilized management technique we used in our company in an atmosphere of calm, and one day Alan and I decided to give it a try at home.

The "Good and Welfare" protocol calls for the individual in question to listen to the issues, not comment or interrupt in any way, and take notes if desired. When the presentation of issues is complete, it is time to respond. This may take the form of asking questions to further explore the problem, agreeing or disagreeing with what the presenter had to say, providing an explanation or some kind of clarification of intention, suggesting a solution ... most anything that feels appropriate relative to the presented issues. The primary purpose of the meeting is to resolve the issues through conversation and with civility. The goal is not to dwell on them and most definitely to move forward. At the end, the list is torn up and thrown away, wiping the slate clean. "Good and Welfare" is not about character attacks or one-sided criticism. It is a constructive outlet so things don't build up without an outlet at all but rather are brought forward in a state of calm and constructiveness. It is really about understanding and growth. For Alan and me, it was a powerful vehicle in finding our way through our marriage, the only difference between how it is conducted at the office and the way we do it at home being the big hug and kiss at the end.

As mentioned earlier, Alan has always been a consistent personality. There are no surprises. He's very predictable, and you know exactly what he's thinking by the way he looks at you and/or the way he communicates his thoughts to you. Alan's thoughts, words, and actions are evolved—a far cry from the man in my first marriage, who'd sulk and not talk to me for two weeks at a time, never letting me in on what I'd done wrong that particular time. With Alan, I have always felt secure and confident, sure of who I was and where I stood, both in the office and in our marriage.

With all of his civility, however, he is very much a man who feels things deeply (I am so fortunate!). Because I'm Cuban and grew up around wild and colorful celebrations, including lively weekend gatherings with relatives, I really love to get out there and dance. It's in my genes. It is not in Alan's. Music doesn't move or even please him the way it does many people, to the point that our daughter Lauren used to force him to identify songs on the car radio when she was a child and tease him when he could not. He'd sit there, driving along, completely stumped. He didn't (and doesn't) even know classic Beatles songs. When we go away or attend a local function, if there's a DJ or band, I need to get up and dance. At one event, a salsa aficionado pulled me up from my seat, and I basically took the lead. Salsa is a very seductive dance with a lot of hip action, and I didn't miss a beat. Mr. Salsa was overwhelmed by my sense of rhythm, not realizing until it was over—when I told him—that maybe my ability to gyrate had to do with the fact that I was as Cuban as he was!

Paramount to that, Alan's expression matched the color of his sea-green tie. As evolved as he is, somehow he didn't appreciate what Mr. Salsa and I were doing, and though it was completely innocent, I kind of liked that. Alan is exquisite. He's the epitome of civility, but he's also human. He is vulnerable and fallible. Not a week passes when I don't think that I've won the jackpot, and he tells me he feels the same way about me too. I'm not sure who we were to each other in past lives, what obstacles or battles we may have faced as family, friends, enemies, or whoever we were to one another, but in this lifetime we've clearly fought and won it all—together.

BUT REALLY ... WHO *IS* THIS HE MARRIED?

Though typically associated with war, PTSD is an insidious condition that possesses the sufferer like a strangling spirit. Think Linda Blair in 1973's *The Exorcist*, only she got help and got out. After the kidnapping (and I will talk about this more in the next chapter), I thought I'd never feel "normal" again; for a long, long time I didn't know I needed help to do that, and when I finally understood that I did, for many long, dark months I didn't know where to turn.

Alan had married a hard-charging executive—a senior officer who'd worked her way up, shown what she was made of, made key decisions, and could take control of most any situation. Except, apparently, her own. When Lauren and I were kidnapped, the residual effects upended everything in my life and, with no other way to put it, unhinged my soul. It came close to unhinging Alan as well, from the standpoint that he had no idea how to help me. The trauma of the kidnapping, the minutes and hours ticking away in the stifling trunk of the car, rendered me powerless over my own life for a very long time—two years, in fact—until I figured out what I needed to do with what had happened to me, again something I will delve into further in chapter 5.

But for now, suffice it to say I became a kind of zombie with extreme body pain (in the places I was holding all the trauma), unable to work, racked with fear and anxiety, remaining in bed for days on end, succumbing to crying jags, unable to function. Somehow I knew God had not let me live only to subsist, being half-alive like this. Alan—almost as undone as I was over the fact that I was falling apart—never did what a lot of men would do in situations where they are rendered powerless for long periods of time, which is to leave. He knew there had to be something else for me and us.

A man characteristically believes he is on the earth to solve and fix it—anything and everything. A woman can sit by and listen, providing support in precisely that way that is quite powerful in itself, but men need to say something, do something, and fix it. Try as he might, Alan could not fix what was wrong with me, though again, much to his credit, he did not write the marriage and me off, just because he couldn't. Alan lived with the flesh-and-blood roller coaster I'd become for a very long time. I was no longer the same person he'd known from a business perspective, and he was trying to figure out how he was going to exist with me from any perspective. I absolutely know it. When Lauren and I were put into that trunk, Alan later told me he'd believed that even if we survived, we could both be so-called basket cases for the rest of our lives, as crime victims bear scars. He may have thought he was prepared, as Alan is for a lot of things, but who is ever prepared for an unknown like that—something they didn't know could ever conceivably present itself? Those kinds of things happen on TV and in the movies, not to you and your family.

Lauren, by the grace of God, had come out unscathed. To this day I don't know if it was God or the angels or possibly the hide-and-go-seek game I told her we were playing when they forced us into the trunk, keeping up the ruse along with a supply of stories and songs as though she were just going for a nap, but she never showed any signs of mental or emotional fallout. She never hesitated to open the front door when the doorbell rang, never suffered psychological issues then or in later years—absolutely nothing!

I, on the other hand, did a nosedive into the abyss—riddled with rage and fear, anxiety and hopelessness, fluctuating between holding on by my bloody fingertips and succumbing to outright insanity. What I went through was incomprehensible. I, however, knew on another level that what I'd clearly gone through was a soul shift.

Alan never left me.

CHAPTER 5

POST-TRAUMATIC STRESS LEADS TO A PORTAL

Out of suffering have emerged the strongest souls; the
most massive characters are seared with scars.

KAHLIL GIBRAN

n the late 1980s, PTSD was not as common a term as it currently is, or if it was, I didn't hear or think much about it. In fact, the first mention of the term was reportedly in 1980, in the third edition of the *Diagnostic and Statistical Manual of Mental Disorders*, published by the American Psychiatric Association.[2] In earlier wars, PTSD was called by different names, including "war neurosis" and "soldier's heart." But whatever the era, the condition

2   http://displus.sk/DSM/subory/dsm3.pdf Category: Anxiety disorders. Code: 308.30 and 3089.81. Page 236.

was largely attributed to returning servicemen who'd experienced the horrors of war, leaving severe mental and physical manifestations and ongoing afflictions.

Somehow I felt as though I'd been through a war, one I was still living and reliving. No matter how someone gets to the point of PTSD, there is typically intense, ongoing psychological and/or physical pain and a numbness or robotic way of experiencing life without understanding why or what's really going on. Nightmares and night sweats—even "daymares," so to speak, are common as the sufferer revisits the traumatic event(s) over and over until he or she is entirely drained and consumed by fear and anxiety. Consumed is a euphemism for what I was going through. I was being eaten alive.

Though Alan had not been forced into the trunk with Lauren and me, he'd lived through what could have been the last night of his life and the very real threat of losing us, yet he displayed no residual effects. He was not walking around in an emotional maelstrom and certainly displaying nothing close to a breakdown. I was teetering on the edge. As for Lauren, maybe because she was so young and I'd used every cell in my body to make what was happening to us into a game for her, she also experienced no effects of trauma. In fact, she never had a fear of anyone breaking in or walking into the house with guns, as the perpetrators had done when they carried out their crime. Her life went on as though nothing out of the ordinary had ever happened to her. If anything, it gave me solace at that point, and for years into the future as she grew up without any scars, it was my knowing I had somehow managed to shield her in those dark, suffocating, fateful hours that I was certain were our last.

When we'd emerged from the trunk, freed by Alan and the bank president, not knowing exactly what to do, Alan had driven us to the drive-through of a Burger King across the street for cold drinks and food and then to a nearby motel to cool us down completely in the air-conditioning. In the limp, dehydrated condition in which he'd found us, he could not have driven us an hour all the way home to Miami. The police and FBI had surrounded and entered the bank by that time, unsure of where we were, with a hoard of bank employees and customers all over the place, so going into the bank was not a wise choice, though he did drive us into the parking lot at first. There, reporters swarmed our car—tipped off by the police scanner—refusing to let us drive out until Alan threatened to run down one of them who'd bodily blocked our egress.

After we pulled into the motel and had taken a little while to cool down, have a little food and drink, and regroup as much as possible, we let the authorities know where we were. This was followed by an afternoon of intense questioning. They separated us, asking the same questions over and over, perhaps in slightly different ways, trying to trip us up in the event we'd actually masterminded the crime and subsequent disappearance of $250,000 in cash. When we told them we'd had a family ski trip planned to Vail in two more days and were intent upon keeping it, the very idea cast a dark shadow over us, making us persons of interest—as though we were planning to abscond with the money. But through it all I was nothing short of robotic. Yes, I sat there for hours, responding to an unrelenting list of questions, though it felt (if I felt anything at all) as though someone else were doing the talking. In retrospect, this made us even more suspect in the eyes of the police, because neither my daughter, nor my husband, nor I were hysterical, sitting in a heap, crying our eyes out, presumably the way most victims react to a crime.

The only thing I left out when recounting the crime to the police and FBI was what happened to me in the trunk. I'm not sure why I left it out, because at the time of the trauma I did not have the analytical skills to make a decision about what they should and should not hear. But I'm glad I told them nothing about my near-death experience lest they decided I was on drugs or mentally imbalanced and carted me off to a psychiatric hospital. The fact is, I had experienced severe trauma and was in shock. My mind and body felt totally disconnected, and the way I conducted myself was simply what was left of me to give.

At some point during the long afternoon, I began to think of Petrona—our beloved housekeeper/nanny who'd gone through this with us. Alan told me the police had gone to our home in Coral Gables, finding her tied to a sliding-glass shower door in a downstairs bathroom. We'd later learn from her that she'd been on her knees the whole time, praying to God for our safe return home.

When the police and FBI finally finished their questioning, we were released and sent on our way. I'd been trying not to think about driving back to Coral Gables. We pulled into the driveway—the same one we had left at the crack of dawn—and got out of the car, and Alan unlocked the front door. Lauren ran to Petrona, and they hugged one other, at which point my legs collapsed underneath me. In my mind's eye, I immediately saw the gunmen in the foyer, and that was all I could see. I began sobbing uncontrollably. "Oh my God," was all I could mutter. Alan tried to gather me up.

"I can't stay here," I told him, pleading. He rushed up the stairs to put together a few things. I followed slowly, peering into the laundry hamper to try to locate a sentimental necklace I'd hidden in the dirty clothes, hoping the kidnappers had not found it when they'd taken our jewelry the night before. It was still there, and I breathed a sigh of relief—practically the only relief about anything I'd feel for months and months to come. I helped Alan pile a few items into a suitcase and turned around as fast as I could, fleeing down the stairs, almost falling down them, and running back into the car.

Alan drove both of us to a Marriott, leaving Lauren—who appeared unscathed by any of this—in Petrona's loving care. He deposited me into bed as soon as we checked in. All I wanted to do was sleep, but that would prove impossible. Every time I closed my eyes, I was back in the trunk. Or I'd open them and close them again, and I was running down the hill, away from the gunmen, as I'd attempted to do the night before when we'd returned home and they were already in our house. Consequently, closing my eyes was not a good thing to do.

The next day Alan's and my parents and the other children came to see us at the hotel. We had a full conversation—almost full—as Alan and I wanted to spare the children many of the details, and then we all watched the news. During the television broadcast, it was the first time Lauren heard the word *kidnapped* and luckily had no clue what it meant. Also, no one spoke about the articles that were published in all the different local newspapers that day. I just sat there, glazed over, zombielike, with no energy and certainly no emotion. Something was deeply wrong, and nothing felt as though it was changing for the better for me.

The children were all packed, eager to get to the airport the next day for our trip to Vail. I couldn't wait to get out of Florida, yet I didn't want to leave. It was a strange juxtaposition of "Am I here? Am I there? Where am I, exactly? What do I want?"

Through my deep emotional pain and confusion and the physical pain in my body that was tearing me apart, Alan's and my parents kept saying, "Thank God they didn't hurt you. Thank God you're fine." Of course, from the outside I looked "fine," but I wasn't feeling any of the kind of "fine" they were talking about. They were completely clueless about my suffering. I could not discuss what had really happened in the trunk, either physically, mentally, or spiritually, because we were trying to keep the kids from knowing that kind of information. We had both made a decision not to panic them in any way—not to traumatize *them* the way I apparently now was. But with that, I was imploding.

When we got on the plane the next day, two nights' sleep had now eluded me—the first when the criminals held us hostage in our house and the second in the hotel, where closing my eyes and reliving things had been almost as agonizing as the actual events themselves. I was still quiet, disconnected, going through the motions—and even that was an effort. Alan would squeeze my hand or try to engage me in family banter, but it was as though I had no blood flowing through me. My lifeless brain and body were being dragged through the ropes, and I was lying in the middle of the ring, defeated before I'd begun—anything. All I could think about was landing in Denver, pushing myself through the two-hour drive to Vail, and going to bed. It was all too much. My head was scrambled. I just wanted to get under the covers and go away. I was forcing myself to do everything. The forcing of it, I think, only added to my pain, because I could not let anything go. I could not release anything. My feelings of distress and despair mounted by the minute. Alan (having put the event behind him, so to speak, in a separate mental compartment) and the children were in a whole different space—raring to get out and go. Any opportunity to be with our combined families excited me, so what was wrong? Alan was essentially straddling both worlds, becoming my caregiver and trying to remain true to our mission: to give the children a close, loving, combined family vacation. He took them to get their ski equipment and register them for ski school right after he poured me into bed. This wonderful man had known me for sixteen years as a serious businessperson and for three months as a caring wife. Of course, we'd gone through an adjustment to being married, as I talked about in the last chapter, but we'd gotten on the right path.

I was now unable to communicate. I was lethargic and disassociated, and to compound things, my body ached like nothing I'd ever felt before—as though it were in a vise. I could not get comfortable on the plane despite the mound of pillows the flight attendants had given me. Ibuprofen did nothing. My head pounded and my muscles clenched, seemingly permanently, feeling leaden at the same time. My back felt as though someone had capped it in cement. It was all so excruciating.

Alan took care of ordering dinner for the children, after which they all showered and kissed me good night. He told them I just wasn't feeling well. The next morning, he took them off to their activities and returned to see about me. I tried to get up while he was there to use the bathroom, and I could not walk. My legs would not move. I don't know how else to describe it except as a kind of paralysis. I tried to force things to move and fell to the floor—just like someone who'd been in an accident. I literally crawled on my belly to the bathroom, calling out to Alan at the top of my lungs. He came running—he didn't expect to see me on the floor—and helped me up onto the john.

"It's shutting down," I remember saying to him through tears, riddled with fear. "My body is stopping and shutting down." I couldn't believe the fact that I was now paralyzed both mentally and physically.

With all that was going on, I was trying hard to remain calm, trying to breathe slowly and evenly. Alan asked me what I thought about going downstairs, trying to break the spell, so to speak, and he helped me dress so I could try. He'd seen a sports physical therapy clinic nearby and a sign advertising massage.

I clung to him and proceeded to take baby steps. A cane would have been a good idea at that point, as without it I could only progress a few inches at a time. My legs were literally numb. When you think about emotional numbness, or mental paralysis maybe, now my body seemed to be taking its cue from my brain, reflecting what I was feeling down to my core. Everything was involved. In a more comprehensive analysis, figuratively and now literally, I was unable to move forward in my life: I was going to have to learn how to live again.

Much later, through a lot of soul searching, counseling, and opening myself to receive what the universe had provided to me, I would come to understand that based on my near-death experience, and as I first mentioned in chapter 1, my whole being was dying at that point. My life as I'd known it for thirty-eight years would never be the same. I was on a new path, though I did not know it in the days, weeks, and first very long months that followed the kidnapping. My brain and body were dying off, preparing to receive new information that would change the course of my life and in some ways the lives of others. It was all ahead of me, but it was nothing I could have ever anticipated.

For now, what was happening to me was so incomprehensible, so extreme, it frightened me to no end. In all of my life I did not recall having back pain or problems walking. I never went through extreme sleep deprivation or this kind of fear and anxiety. I was not a functioning human being.

When Alan and I arrived at the clinic for the massage, he asked if there was a particular therapist who could address the extreme pain I was in. A woman who was said to specialize in this kind of thing came out, took me into a room, and asked me to disrobe and climb onto the massage table. She left so I could do so privately. I was so disconnected I do not recall complying, but I must have. She returned and instructed me to lie face down, dimming the lights and dialing in some relaxing music. She placed a chair at the head of the table and began working on my neck. Next she went around to my back, her hands floating above it, remarking that she felt intense heat coming from it. When she laid her hands on my back, I jumped up like a jack-in-the-box, almost right off the table. I wrapped the sheet that had gently covered part of me all the way around me, breaking into deep, unrelenting sobs. It was almost as though she had done something to hurt me, though clearly she had not. She had keyed in on a part of my body that had been holding the trauma, and I was hysterical. There were sounds coming out of me I did not recognize. Somehow she had tapped into the depths of my anguish, which was now pouring out of me. I remember how gentle and compassion-ate she was, holding me as a parent would an inconsolable child. I leaned my head on her shoulder, awash in tears that seemed to have no beginning and no end. She and I remained in that position for the entire rest of the session as my body proceeded to try to release whatever had it in a stranglehold. She did no more work on me, as my being held, and feeling it was safe to cry with her seemed to be exactly what was needed.

At some point during the hour, she asked me softly if I wanted to talk about whatever had happened. I told her I did not but that I would come back the next day and maybe I would be able to talk then.

I did return the next day, and the day after that. While I'd still been unable to sleep, I was taking catnaps but to the best of my knowledge never entering the deep REM sleep where we dream, necessary for all of us to function. If I let myself sleep any longer than a few minutes, there he was—standing in the foyer of my house with his weapon pointed at us. The massage therapist seemed willing to listen, just as patient and kind as she'd been the previous day, so I told her what had happened in the trunk. She confirmed that I'd been holding the trauma in my back and that it had lodged there to such a degree, it impacted everything else. I gave her additional details about the position I'd been in in the trunk with Lauren. Over the next two or three days, she did all she could on my back and legs, and I felt a bit better physically. But it was short-lived. It wasn't anything that stayed with me, because I'd not dealt with my trauma or anything on an emotional level.

BACK IN BATTLE MODE

When we got back to Florida, Alan and I returned to our temporary living quarters at the Marriott with Lauren. I didn't know what we were going to do from there, but I was certain I was never going back to that home—the home my two girls and I had lived in for the past six years. Our suite had a couch, and I'd periodically sit there with Alan, still emotional and crying, trying to tell him what happened to Lauren and me in the trunk, over and over, trying to get him to understand why I was in this condition, so fraught with fear and anxiety. I'm not sure why I felt compelled to repeat the tale so much, except that maybe I thought there would be one pivotal moment where he'd suddenly jump up, proclaiming that he got it, and not only that he got it but that he fully understood it. While he was infinitely patient and deeply compassionate, that strongly hoped-for moment never occurred. What had happened to me was truly inexplicable and complicated for anyone to understand. And there was more.

"Listen," I said to him one night. "I know we just got married. I know you were expecting me to continue doing what I was doing, but there is no way I can go back to work with you. I cannot go back to being COO of the company. It is not where I belong." We'd been working together for about sixteen years at that point, and as much as I loved what I had been doing, I firmly believed I was not left alive—with the miracle I'd experienced—to take up the same kind of life I'd been living as though nothing had ever happened. I was acutely aware of that.

"I understand," Alan said, almost without hesitation. I'm not sure he did at all, but I had married someone with enough heart for a million men. "I'll support whatever you want to do. You do what you need to do." I was not returning to my home and now also not returning to the job I loved. My personal and professional life had been upended and beyond turned upside down.

I knew at least enough by that point to understand that what had happened had pulled the rug out from under me in the most powerful way. I was lying on the floor. There was nothing left of me, or left to chance, or deliberation, or the choice of getting to weigh this option against that one. I knew I was not the same person, not the same being who had gone to the other side. I had come back as a different creature entirely. My energy had shifted, and my life's plan was no longer what I thought it was going to be. I was still in a state of total craziness, but if one ounce of clarity was available to me, it was that the road had forked, and I was being catapulted down the alternate route.

LEAVING THE SCENE OF THE CRIME

During the three months we lived at the hotel, Alan drove Lauren back and forth to school and went to work. I counted some very long hours alone with my thoughts, running like an old gangster movie over and over in my head. Occasionally I'd reach out to family members (other than Alan) about what was going on inside me, but my laments were always met with the same response: "Come on, dear, nothing physical happened to you. Just look at yourself. You're fine." Their observations—clearly well-intentioned (but unenlightened) about a desperate situation—only served to fuel the rage inside of me. I felt like a victim, a trapped animal. I was *not* fine. I just didn't know what to do with it all. In my head I was yelling, *Help me, please—I am not okay.*

I had many conversations with my husband about needing security. I had no one to turn to except him—someone so busy now being both father and mother to Lauren, being both CEO of a bank and NYSE public company and scouting out a new home for us. He hired a broker to look for the kind of house he knew I needed. My criteria included the constant physical presence of guards. I wanted twenty-four-hour armed guards right outside the door. The house needed to have a huge, impenetrable gate around it with an intercom. Home-surveillance video cameras were not a lot in use then, or I'd have had them as well, spaced about a foot apart.

When a viable, secure residence was found, I felt badly, as Petrona, who had been living at the old house, had to pack all of us and the entire house up by herself with occasional help from Alan when he could break away and drive over there. I was mentally and physically in no condition to spend days and maybe weeks in that space doing it. I'm a Virgo, and perfection is my middle name, so typically the way I pack is a tour de force of organization, but at that time what mattered most was getting as far away as fast as possible from the scene of the crime.

"SAMMAGE" AND SUZANNE

We finally moved to our new secure home, which got us out of a hotel and physically removed me from what had become the nightmare surroundings of my former home. But as the saying goes, "We cannot get away from ourselves." The fear, rage, and anxiety continued to build inside me. I was impotent in so many ways. I went from spending every day in bed at the hotel to spending every day in bed at our new home—I was still numb and frozen. I just couldn't move. For the most part, I would not allow anyone to come over socially, as every time someone appeared at the gate and the intercom announced a presence, I was hurled back to the dark hours at gunpoint or in the trunk. It was horrible on everyone.

What was happening? Why was I living my life like this? What circumstances had painted me into this miserable, hermitic corner, and for what reason? Surely, I'd not been in the presence of angels only to come back and live in hell. I asked myself these and a hundred other related questions over and over and over, day in and day out.

During this time, one of the security guards actually became my daughter Lauren's favorite playmate as he amused her when she played outside the house. She was unable to have friends over because of her mother's fragility, jumping at doorbells and strangers in the house. Alan's teenage children would come over from time to time, of course—the children I also considered mine when we'd gotten married because I loved them so much—but I was generally unable to interact with them … or anyone else.

Sometimes, if I got out of bed, Alan and I would be alone in the kitchen on a weekend. I would be a mess, telling him I needed help—needed *something*—that I knew deep in my heart that I could not heal by myself, that I was sure he could just not understand the immense pain I went through and was still living. I was sure what he'd gone through with the kidnappers did not compare to what I'd endured. How could he know the kind of mental, emotional, and physical pain I was in? He had been able to move on from whatever happened to him and was busy doing his job, raising the children, managing the household, and everything else I had unwittingly abandoned to be as sick as I was. I was angry, hurt, upset, isolated, buried alive. I was frozen in time—a prisoner of my travails. I lived in total darkness. I groped and clawed and couldn't find the light. How could I have been in the magnificent company of angels in a near-death experience, seeing the light, and then be sent back and now stuck in this quagmire of madness, depression, and posttraumatic stress?

At one point, in his efforts to help someone he loved out of a situation with which he had no idea how to cope and solve, Alan engaged a massage therapist to come to the house each week. The one in Vail seemed to have had a positive effect on me, though it didn't last, and he thought perhaps I would again relate to something like that. Because Lauren had trouble with the word *massage*, she'd let me know the "sammage" lady was in the house as the woman lugged her table up the stairs. She did her best, but like the massage therapist in Vail, any good feelings were short-lived. In a day or two I was back in pain—in my own hell, as it were.

It was now August of 1989. I'd essentially been paralyzed like this since the crime in December of the previous year. I almost never left the house. We'd had Wackenhut security outside the front door twenty-four seven, and I still lived in abject terror of someone getting inside. I was drowning in fear. I'm not sure why getting counseling had not occurred to us, except that no one in either of our families had ever seen a therapist. It wasn't something that ever came to mind … until one day in late summer when it did occur to us. Alan made some calls in search of a recommendation of a good therapist. Somehow, when he made the appointment, though I knew nothing about this psychotherapist, a modicum of the burden I'd been carrying was lifted, and I said I'd try to drive myself there. Getting behind the wheel had been out of the question for me even on the rare occasions I had ventured out, as I always felt fearful, weak and disoriented. But with everything on Alan's plate, I was now determined to do this for myself. I couldn't let the way I felt destroy me (or him) any longer.

I was happy to have made it to the appointment safe and sound. I don't know what it was about the questions the therapist asked me, but though I sat through it to the end, I ran out the door in tears. I barely heard him say he wanted to set up our next appointment as I was running out to the car. He had obviously tapped into something I felt was brutally painful. I made it a few blocks toward home but then pulled over to the side of the road, crying my eyes out. I thought, *Well, what now? Nobody's ever going to be able to fix me. Wow … am I going to be the way I am forever?* I told Alan that the therapist was the wrong one for me, but who or what was going to be right?

Later that night, in total despair and desperation, I prayed, asking God for help.

"God, I know deep in my heart, deep in my soul, this is not what you wanted me to come back to, to sit and suffer the rest of my life, to not participate with my family and my husband, or do what you saved me to do." I recall falling asleep and having a very odd dream—I wasn't having many dreams up till then. In the dream, I was supposed to go get a manicure (that's right—a manicure!) at some salon in South Miami on Saturday, a salon where I'd never been before. I got the feeling I was supposed to meet somebody there—somebody who would begin to factor deeply into my life.

Strange as it was, I decided to start paying attention to things like this, as it might be the answer to my prayer. At that point I'd not gotten a lot of information coming through me because my mind and body were all locked up. But this very powerful message had come through in a basic dream form, and my instincts told me to heed it.

On Saturday, I asked Alan to take me and to just sit and relax in the waiting area while I was getting a manicure. My love did not ridicule me. He didn't laugh or call me crazy—or say he knew I was crazy and now I was even crazier. He simply asked what little I could tell him about the salon and its possible location. Somehow, I knew it was in the Red Road, South Miami area, but not much more. He was kind enough to drive me around so I could key in on its location. When I recognized the salon from my dream, I went inside. I was taken to one of the manicurists and seated at her workspace, next to another customer. I looked at the customer and knew immediately I was supposed to introduce myself. The dream had guided me to do that, though I had no idea why. But I did know it was the sole reason I was there.

Suzanne didn't think my introducing myself to her was strange at all. In our first brief conversation, I asked her what she did for a living. She revealed that she was a pastoral counselor and hypno-therapist. I had no idea what a pastoral counselor was and was wary of hypnotherapy, where I felt I'd lose control, but Suzanne was about to give me my life back … a decidedly different life. With her help I was about to step out of the darkness through a very special portal reserved just for me.

CHAPTER 6

FIRST LIGHT!

When you die and go to heaven our maker is not going to ask,
"Why didn't you discover the cure for such and such? Why didn't
you become the Messiah?" The only question we will be asked
in that precious moment is "Why didn't you become you?"

ELIE WIESEL

once saw the term *spiritual gangster*. It was actually on a T-shirt, and I bought it because it spoke to me. While it could be misconstrued as something forceful in a negative way (referencing Al Capone or Ma Barker, maybe), the way I see it, a spiritual gangster is someone getting out there and living a fearless life—a life infused with the faith that we are guided and supported in our most challenging pursuits. In vernacular, it's just going for it.

At this juncture in my life, the most I was hoping for was to be able to string together two or three days in a row where I felt safe and "normal" again, where I could close my eyes over the course of a few nights and not see the faces of the people who did this to me, or where I could leave my house and not feel as though someone was waiting for me steps away from the security guard so they could finish the job. Up to that point I was caught up in all the fear and negativity, going down a rabbit hole, spiraling down where everyone and everything felt like they were against me. I was in a deep and dark place of hopelessness.

I didn't want to continue to feel as though I'd been run over (and over) by a Mack truck, and maybe paramount to that, I wanted to rejoin my family in celebrating each and every day we tried to spend together. I wanted to stand at the stove and help Alan make his specialty cinnamon French toast, matzah brei, or egg in the basket when all the kids were over with their friends, without feeling as though I were about to collapse into a disoriented heap. I wanted to be a real partner to my husband again. I wanted to be able to assume some responsibility in my marriage and home. That would have been enough spiritual gangster for me—at least for the time being.

When I met Suzanne at the salon, she'd told me she was a pastoral counselor and hypnotherapist. Again, I had no idea what a pastoral counselor was and wasn't too keen on being put under hypnosis. Losing control is an issue for a lot of people; as a control freak and with the kind of corporate power I'd had for a long time, it certainly was for me. But given my very vivid and powerful dream, I felt compelled to get her phone number, asking if we could talk later when we'd both gotten home.

We ended up talking for three hours about what she does, how she does it, and how she helps clients shift and heal. I learned that pastoral counseling involves facilitating healing through spiritual and other realms and life-changing conversations. Where hypnotherapy is concerned, she had such a beautiful way of describing the process. I had to trust it would probably be okay. I told Alan, "That's the woman from my dream that I'm supposed to go heal with." She lived in Kendall, thirty to forty-five minutes away, but geography didn't matter. I'd have driven a lot farther to be with her, as I immediately set up my first appointment and then began seeing her once and soon twice a week. Each time I went, I told her she was a defining and transformational gift from the universe. And I meant it. She gave me clarity. She was patient, loving, and compassionate. Her home office, where we met, was cozy, comfortable, and sun filled. When I looked out the window to take a breath before speaking, I could see the beautiful purple bougainvillea tree blooming outside. Often I would just sit and bask in the light and the silence for a while, and she supported my doing that.

She inspired and impacted me. Suzanne was not only a catalyst for empowerment; she helped me dig deep for, find, and connect with my feelings and emotions.

I said early on that I had been very much a "doing" rather than a "being" kind of person. I was a typical "corporation man." But now I had to find the courage to open myself up, maybe like the pages of a book. My internal book. I needed the courage to open myself up *unlike anything I had ever done before.* We are creatures of habit, and to compound that, I had been to the depths. Laying myself open was terrifying at times, but at the same time, with Suzanne it was always safe.

Suzanne and I talked about a panoply of things over six months, becoming very close in the process. In relationships and in life, being able to trust the people with whom we surround ourselves is essential. With Suzanne, my change agent, I always felt understood and secure.

The ability to trust reinforces our faith and gives us peace of mind. I was also learning how to trust myself and what was coming through me on a deeper spiritual level—not knowing then that I was being guided. I began to feel my energy shift. I was now vibrating at a higher frequency. Lights, portable phones, televisions, radios—anything electronic—were not my friends. My new energy field created all sorts of unique and unusual experiences, and I couldn't explain what this was or why this was happening.

Suzanne connected the dots. She used to say to me, "We cannot become ourselves by ourselves." She was right. This is an underlying tenet in pastoral counseling, and maybe counseling in general. It is why you seek someone out professionally, and if you find the right person, she can give you possibilities, inspiration, and motivation. You can't always do that by yourself, especially if you're in trauma or depressed, as I was.

Each session with Suzanne nudged me further and further into the promise of my new life—all it could hold—creating a path for more peace and balance. There was room for joy and gratitude to show up again, maybe more than ever before, and for forgiveness to emerge in a new way. I was beginning to feel more truly awakened at the highest level, strong and courageous, with direction and a new story.

I confided in Suzanne my lifelong dream to go to college—and I would go, even much further than I thought. Suzanne taught me that everything is part of the human journey with a divine plan, that my thoughts and experiences were valid and ordained on the spirit plane. Nothing is ever wasted, as it is part of God's plan for us.

Difficult times, dark times, are when we learn to trust in Him/Her and to persevere.

Suzanne directed me to read books on near-death experiences. These books fed me. I was relieved to see how so many other people who'd had near-death experiences felt, experiencing the same things I had! There is knowledge and great comfort in numbers. I finally found my kumbaya group in those books.

Because of the kind of work she did, under hypnotherapy I had some amazing "aha" moments: messages, lessons, and realizations that had come from the beings when I was on the other side. It all came pouring out. Suzanne taught me that fear is irrelevant. No more worries. No more struggles. She kept reminding me how strong and resilient I was, how to move on with grace and courage. Cliché or otherwise, she kept saying that everything happens for a reason. *Everything.* "It happened, and here you are," she'd say, "*right now*. Remember the present moment." As more and more time passed in my sessions with Suzanne, I learned that I needed to be dismantled so I could be rebuilt. I was now connecting with what would be my new "superpowers."

Not to boast, but the knowledge, buried treasure, and talents she would free in me were all part of the reason I'd needed to go through the kidnapping. Because of my life review, I came to understand it— unbelievably enough, even embrace it—to essentially forgive what the experience did to me. I had to stop punishing myself for all the feelings of being a victim that kept me stuck. I had to forgive myself. I had to forgive my perpetrators. I had to find new meaning and uncover qualities and capabilities that would give me a new, vibrant, and truly purposeful life. I had to remember the gifts I had been shown and given. My new destiny.

And perhaps this was another lesson: as much of a challenge as it was, I had to glean profoundly positive meaning from a profoundly negative event.

I also had to learn self-forgiveness, self-love, patience, empathy—and really *how* to forgive. What did that mean? What form did that take?

While I was not a bad person to begin with, I clearly walked the earth with my eyes glued shut. If it didn't appear in an interoffice communication, I probably didn't see it. When I'd had my life review during the near-death experience, all this had become crystal clear to me. Suzanne reinforced it and opened doors for me to learn another way of being, giving me a new perspective on what my thoughts, words, and actions had been up to that moment.

The fact is, the real *essence* of qualities such as self-love, patience, empathy (and again, self-forgiveness—I can't emphasize this enough!) was somewhat foreign to me. I did not practice them on a daily basis and therefore was not in touch with them. I had to build on my new foundation. Suzanne motivated me. My family is the primary reason I needed to come back from a very dark place, and Suzanne showed me how to step forward into the light with the new gifts I had been given during my near-death experience.

We all go through difficult times. Coping with challenges, we develop a new level of self-confidence, self-acceptance, and trust in ourselves. But with all of that comes a vulnerability that is important too, though we fight to conceal it when the world routinely tells us to toughen up. It's what makes us unconditionally human, though, and I learned that it was all right for me to show up imperfectly—or as I was now—in the world.

It was all right for me not to have all the answers and openly admit it when I didn't. We come to earth in a physical body to serve one another and certainly to love, which is the *only* emotion that we take back with us when we die. When I began to understand this, there was a euphoria I only wished everyone could have ... and I still do. I think it is possible to find this level of understanding about our purpose on earth without having a near-death experience as I did.

Suzanne taped everything, because when under hypnosis, you are not constrained by what you are saying, and she couldn't write it down fast enough. It was important for me to replay the sessions and hear what had transpired. I came to understand how essential fully expressing all of the deep emotions and fears I'd felt were to my healing process. The information I got from the tapes was both unforgettable and life changing.

Even with that, the healing happened very slowly. I was changing, just not aware of it as it was occurring. Maybe it was like a large bucket of rain where the drops accumulate almost imperceptibly, but one day you turn around and there's enough to quench your thirst for a long time and sustain you.

Six months into my work with Suzanne, I found myself mentally, physically, and spiritually embracing my true self. It felt like I was finally in a stable place. I was at peace. Spiritual revelation is far beyond anything I can comprehend or even really describe. I was finally rested and refreshed. I was absolutely certain my time with Suzanne was a gift that had been sent to me from God, and I was grateful every day that I'd paid attention to the enigmatic dream about the nail salon. Paying attention, being open and aware, listening for clues, guidance—it all comes in many forms. It could be a book that falls off a shelf, a song on the radio, a chance reunion on the street, or a casual remark made by someone in passing. I learned that paying attention would be the key that unlocked so much in my life, in spiritual matters and tangible ones as well.

That was actually just the beginning of my trusting information that was coming through me and being open to the healing that came as a result. It was the start of my trusting spiritual information—or what is more commonly called intuition.

One day, two or three years after the 1988 kidnapping and near-death experience that provided the foundation for my life's work, Alan and I were called to Los Angeles, where the mastermind had been apprehended. We were able to identify him by providing witness testimony in court, and he was subsequently sentenced to a prison term. Apparently he had gone on to perpetrate the same crime on people and families throughout the country. In one case, it ended in murder. A woman—not on trial—was with him in the courtroom, and while I could not be sure, I presumed it could be the woman whose voice I'd heard on the other end of the phone in the bedroom the morning we were put in the trunk. In fact, when Lauren and I were in the trunk, before the car reached its final destination, we had pulled over, and I'd heard what sounded like the doors of a van sliding open. A conversation ensued between the man who was driving us and a woman—again, likely the same woman who'd been on the other end of the phone that morning.

When the trial was over, we flew back to Florida, and frankly I did not think twice about anything more coming of this. But many months later, during a meeting at the bank, I was gripped by something that felt like a sword going through my back and out the front of me. It took my breath away. In an instant I knew the woman was in Florida—coming back for us. Out of the blue, I yelled out—"They're back!" I grabbed Alan and told him. Naturally he was incredulous, dismissive, telling me how inconceivable it was that I would "know" something like this. He refused to pay any attention to the idea or to me about it.

"I'm leaving, and so should you," I told him adamantly. "I'm going home to get Lauren and Petrona, and we're all going to a hotel. I am not going to spend another minute in that house, because she's coming back for us."

The next day the newspaper headlines retold our story. And, in addition, it said that the woman and her accomplices had been apprehended at a small Palm Beach airport, packing weapons and ammunition. As my message undisputedly informed me loud and clear, she had come back to kill us.

From that experience—from that day forward—Alan has never again doubted the messages I receive: my otherworldly "inner knowing."

As good and *relieved* as I was starting to feel, I couldn't help but wonder what I needed to be doing with the rest of my life. What was next? What was I supposed to be? Why was I spared from what for all intents and purposes should have been certain death? What was my purpose now?

LEGIONS OF COMFORT

During my time with Suzanne, in addition to the books on near-death experiences, she'd often suggest some other revolutionary reading. As I was largely still in bed when I started with her, it gave me something to do. Slowly but surely I crawled out for longer periods of time, becoming less of a victim or prisoner, opening up to understanding and unlimited possibilities. The books helped. I felt a strong sense of needing to step fully into my destiny.

Among these books was Dr. Brian Weiss's *Many Lives, Many Masters*, which delved into past-life regression and reincarnation.

An Ivy League–educated traditional psychotherapist for many years, Weiss, though initially skeptical, became quite curious when one of his patients, Catherine, began recalling past-life traumas, which he eventually determined were the key to her recurring nightmares and anxiety attacks. The patient also began channeling very specific details about Dr. Weiss's life, including his twenty-three-day-old infant who'd died of a rare congenital heart deformity, facts that no one could have known about (these were preinternet days). The story goes that from that moment on, the way he practiced therapy was transformed.

I actually went to hear him speak before I read his book, both his presentation and book validating what I'd experienced in my journey to the other side. I knew there were others out there like me who'd been through the tunnel and had seen the guides and the angels and had received telepathic messages. I felt a strong sense of being okay. If you are completely unfamiliar with the metaphysical realm, you can't help but feel you are losing your mind … discombobulated. Coming from corporate America as I had, and as I hope I've presented well enough in this book, the transition had been overwhelming. But now I was on to a startling new and meaningful life. I could feel it! Finding how to use my new skills and talents, life would be a great process of discovery, a challenge I embraced.

HIGHER THOUGHTS; HIGHER EDUCATION

Among the decisions I made at that point was to go to school. I'd been forced to marry Orlando right out of high school, my dreams of higher education thwarted. When that relationship ended and I'd started to climb my way up in business, I'd been fortunate to have taken various courses Norman and Alan had encouraged me to take whenever I'd wanted to, but now this was different. It was all about embarking on a brand new life. I couldn't help but think back to the lost days when Orlando's parents had purchased a large home into which we all moved so his mother could more easily care for little Gina and the sprawling Miami Dade College I'd see as I drove back and forth each day to my job in Orlando's car. As I said in chapter 3, the buildings were a billboard to the future—a neon sign screaming "College! College! College!" and it called to me. Now I could finally go.

I first matriculated at Broward Community College (now Broward College) and then Nova Southeastern University with a major in psychology. While it felt good and right for me, thinking I'd be able to help others in the way Suzanne had helped me, I also listened to my intuition.

Two years into my education at NSU, another psychology major around my age with whom I'd connected, as we were older than the other students, asked me if I'd ever heard of the Florida Religious Studies Institute. I had not. She strongly encouraged me to look into it given my interests in meditation, metaphysics, hypnosis, and pastoral counseling, which I'd shared with her on a few occasions.

Unlike conventional sources for higher education, the Florida Religious Studies Institute had four-year and two-year programs. It was more expansive in its philosophy about learning, allowing me to explore different modalities of psychological and spiritual concepts. Though now defunct, the institute did not offer a degree but rather a certificate, which was exactly what I'd needed to become a nondenominational pastoral counselor. I wanted to follow the guidance that spirit had given me. I was courageously allowing, without questioning, the flow of people and events put into my life to take me wherever I needed to go. I was not really questioning, analyzing, or planning—at least not the way I used to. Certainly by this time, and thanks to the work Suzanne and I did together, I knew my soul comprehended every message and that there was something I was destined to do that was much greater than I was.

BRINGING THE OTHER SIDE HERE

When I enrolled, I learned that part of the education requirement was a year-long internship in the second year. I chose Hospice by the Sea as my milieu. At the time, I knew my mission was to help people cross over to the other side in a peaceful, loving way. I needed to pray with and over them, such as reciting Psalm 23 the way I had in the trunk. I felt then—and in fact I know now more than almost anything—that it is among the most powerful prayers ever. People attach so much fear to dying, largely because it is the unknown. I had been there and knew my role was to let others know the other side was impossibly perfect, filled with love and light, and that they had nothing to fear. Sometimes being on this side was far more daunting than what is in store for us.

Things began to shift and change for me in my understanding of my own self when, all told, I was assigned six different individuals approaching the end of their lives. Their experiences in the transition from life to death were enormously powerful for me. One of my assignments was a woman with breast cancer that had metastasized to her bones and brain. It was everywhere. They'd given her one to two months to live, and she lived for six. I had now taken many classes and workshops and had become a Reiki master. During our time together, I did Reiki on her—a process geared toward stress reduction by activating the body's natural healing. It's a gentle, nonintrusive, hands-on healing technique that uses a spiritual frequency and energy.

My hospice cancer patient and I talked a lot about forgiveness, spirituality, and metaphysical concepts, something I also did with other patients, or perhaps it was just about reading and listening to patients for as long as they wanted. I was there to ease their transition, but there was no doubt that what I got from my hours with each of them gave my life a depth and quality I'd not have otherwise known.

Years earlier at Broward College, I'd had a nice association with a South American math professor I'll call Enrique. We were about the same age and perhaps had more to talk about with me than he would have had with the nineteen-year-olds in the class. Math was never my forte, but it was a requirement, and Enrique gave all he knew to make the class manageable and even pleasant and interesting for me. I passed!

At the time I'd had no idea his father-in-law was ill, and a few years later, during my Florida Religious Studies Institute hospice internship, one of the ongoing home visits I was assigned was his father-in-law's residence. At some point the professor showed up, recognized me, and asked what on earth I was doing there. Talk about synchronicity! He gave me his cell phone number, and one day soon afterward, I called him, telling him to assemble his family and get to the house right away, as it was probably his father-in-law's last day. The following day he called me, thanking me profusely, because the entire family got to be there in the final moments. I was grateful that I'd begun receiving messages about the patients with whom I was working at that time, though these messages were heartbreaking and difficult to deliver to families.

Years later, Alan's father was dying. He had lapsed into a coma and was in a hospice unit in a hospital. We were having Thanksgiving dinner at our house when we got the call to go to his bedside.

But I told Alan his father wanted us not to be there when he passed, something that was distressing to a loving son—so loved and adored by his father—to say the least. We went anyway. After some time had passed, we kissed Alan's father goodbye and drove home. When we arrived, the smoke detector was chirping in the living room. During the drive home, the hospital had called to say he had expired. There was nothing cooking at our house, no wiring issues, just the sound of the chirping. I knew it was Alan's father assuring us he was there with us, and I told Alan so. In a few minutes, the chirping stopped on its own. On the day of the shiva at Alan's parents' (now his mother's) house—the Jewish tradition following burial where family and friends get together to pray, remember the deceased, and provide solace for one another—the smoke detector also starting chirping in the living room for a few minutes in the way it had at our house. I knew Alan's father was there again, watching over us.

THE SOUND OF HEALING

On another occasion, I received clear and specific information through yet another vivid dream. I was to meet someone named Steven Halpern, a Grammy-nominated composer, recording artist, and producer who specializes in healing through music. My husband, Alan, subscribed to multiple local and national newspapers, and I immediately opened the *Sun Sentinel*. There he was in an upper-right-corner half-page ad. You couldn't miss it. Set to appear at the Broward Convention Center, Steven Halpern is known as a "sound healer." Initially I had no idea who he was, anything about his credentials (the internet was still someone's tech dream at this point), or why I was directed to find him, except that I was supposed to work with him on a project. All I knew was that I was supposed to get to him. I trusted the guidance I'd received. I went to hear him play his healing music. When the event was over and while he was packing up his equipment, I knew I was supposed to look into his eyes and say, "I was told by Spirit I am supposed to make a meditation tape with you." That's what my guides in my dream told me to say, so I did it. Maybe a little to my surprise (though only a little by this time), he immediately got what I was saying and proceeded to ask me when I'd like to go into the studio and do this. The result was a tape (later a CD) I channeled, without notes, called *Meditations for a Peaceful Heart.* Guiding words, set to Steven's revolutionary music, flowed through me—maybe *gushed* is a better word—and the finished product was something I could never have envisioned doing (nor would I have wanted to!) before my brand new life.

I had learned to raise my vibration and frequency, something that happens when we meditate consistently so that we are increasingly open to receiving intuitively. What I had activated was rich and undeniable.

My older daughter Gina—who had been grown and out of the house when Alan and I got together, had graduated from the University of Miami, and was now the art director of a design firm—designed the cover art for my meditation tapes, as I didn't stop at one. *Meditations for Healing Stress* followed. I could not stop the flow, and why would I have wanted to?

Not to let everything I'd learned in two decades of my former business life go by the wayside, I tried to figure out how to market my tapes—how to get them into people's hands—because the purpose for my having made them was to provide a guided meditation for relaxation and healing. I'd go door-to-door to New Age stores, where I'd be told they didn't buy directly from individuals. Ultimately I was given the contact information for a distributor of metaphysical material in Georgia. I sent samples of my work, and they took me on. I also had some friends and acquaintances who agreed to feature my tapes in their shops.

When the metaphysical distributor accepted my work, I was told I'd have to produce these tapes on a regular basis. I was on my way to doing what I was apparently supposed to do: bring healing to others the way I'd been healed through the power of meditation.

The darkness was behind me. It was a blessed and fertile time, and I was able to channel two powerful meditation tapes.

Now there was also a book inside of me. I met someone (through a friend) who knew about publishing, whereupon I told him I'd channeled a book on meditation, about earth changes, and more. It was an oracle book, because the work had come through me. I explained that I was not the author but the conduit, the vessel, the instrument. It was not my information, but I believed it needed to get out there. He said he would help me, and Gina worked with me again to design the cover art. I titled it *God Has Your Best Interest at This Time*, obtained the requisite ISBN, and Amazon picked it up. I was also sharing the book and the messages with my Thursday-night meditation group, the thirty-plus-member Women's Wisdom Circle, some of whom also became private clients for my pastoral counseling and Life Coaching. I was beyond pleased that I was making inroads toward sharing the wondrous healing that had taken place for me by having other people benefit from what I'd learned. My purpose was to empower women to shift and change their lives. I was coaching, facilitating, and being of service to women in ways I could not have imagined.

But with all the good in my life now, there was something gnawing at me. Perhaps it was not as much of a gnawing as a knowing.

Was this what God wanted me to do? Was this really it? Was it everything? Or was there more—something else? I lived in the question.

In my (nondenominational) pastoral counseling sessions with private clients, we talked a lot about personal growth and self-development, what to do, where to go, how to be heard. Many of these women were quite sad, having issues with their husbands and/or children and with work-life balance. Sometimes people just need a safe and loving environment, as I'd had with Suzanne, in which to empty themselves and tell the truth, no matter how frightening it can be. It's what had enabled me to climb out of the abyss I'd been in for what had seemed like eternity, and I wanted anyone who desired a richer, gentler, happier life to find their way out of the pain.

THE FUTURE IS NOW

Five years passed, and the question "Should I be doing something more? Different? Something else?" kept at me. I had my meditation tapes, my book, my pastoral counseling, my Life Coaching, and the Women's Wisdom Circle. With everything I'd accomplished, I still and always felt I was the instrument, not the source. Answers and ideas did not originate with me but rather flowed through me. I was honored to have a great number of speaking engagements and radio interviews—I was even on with Howard Stern during this time—upwards of thirty of them, to talk about my near-death experience. I came to understand from this that I had the opportunity to talk about it not from a sad, negative, self-pitying kind of place but rather approaching it from a transformational, life-changing perspective—a perspective of the gift and blessing I'd been given. It was about how healing by getting to the other side of the pain through forgiveness was the key to living a significant life. "I could have remained a victim," I would tell these groups. "I could have been stuck in the darkness, maybe even have gotten physically ill if you subscribe to the mind-body connection. But I was lucky to have been shown a path to the light."

Often at the end of my speech, I'd play the Mariah Carey song "Hero," emphasizing the message that each and every one of us has a hero within if we can just become fearless enough about exposing her. I like to say that you don't have to be afraid of what you are and all that you are. Naturally not everyone cared about my message, but I'd see others leaving at the end, wiping away tears because they'd connected with something. Whatever I was saying was something they'd needed to receive. Whether they realized it or not, that's why they'd come that day. They got it, and it was very empowering for me to be a facilitator of whatever level of healing was taking place for them. The spiritual gangster was off and running.

CHAPTER 7

FINDING—AND FOUNDING—BALANCE

The purpose of our lives is to give birth to the best which is within us.

MARIANNE WILLIAMSON

Somewhere around 1996, when I'd been doing what I was doing for a considerable amount of time and was in a good place, I still hadn't entirely answered the question, What else could I be doing to facilitate healing, maybe to reach a larger audience? News of a New Age conference at the Miami Arena came to me through a friend. I understood there would be an impressive list of presenters and also an opportunity to rent a booth for $500, something my friend said she'd like to split with me. By this time I'd made thousands of copies of my meditation tapes and wanted to get them out there for people to connect with my channeled words and the energetic vibrations from the healing music of Stephen Halpern. Sounded like a good idea to me.

As the universe would have it (of course, there are no accidents), I found myself next to a booth with someone named Susan who published a small New Age magazine of sorts that featured metaphysical topics. It was distributed at Whole Foods.

The fact is, I had been open to the possibility of creating a magazine myself, having presented my dilemma of reaching a broader audience to members of my Women's Wisdom Circle, asking for their input. These women were valued participants in one another's lives, and certainly in mine. I'd created my Women's Wisdom Circle for women who wanted to be part of a group focused on growth and transformation. It was free space—much like the environment in which I'd found myself during my time with Suzanne—where there was no judgment. It was rooted in trust, acceptance, and encouragement. The Women's Wisdom Circle was a space in which to observe and learn from each other. We got together to talk, celebrate, and meditate. We were equals on the journey, coming together to support one another with intention. We got to speak our truths about who we were, no matter what. We listened. We laughed. We expressed compassion and gratitude. We embraced things as they unfolded and evolved. As time went on, we became grounded and centered, learning to care for and nurture ourselves (something women typically do not do) as much as we did the others in the group. We basked in each other's company. So when I approached these women about helping me consider my next steps in promoting healing, I took what they had to say seriously. I knew they had my back.

Along those lines, someone suggested a newsletter, which was heading in the right direction, though it didn't seem to be quite enough for my purposes. I was looking to do something on a larger scale. When someone else proposed a magazine, it was certainly a bigger venture, but I did not consider myself a writer and didn't have a clue about advertising sales and publishing something that comprehensive on a consistent basis. So it was left out there. I was, as the saying goes, living in the question. Eventually I ended the group, as we had been meeting for years and I thought we'd gone as far as we could.

But Susan had a magazine. She and I hit it off conversationally, waiting for convention goers to stop by our respective booths. We decided to take our conversation further by having lunch, as I'd told her I had a lot of business experience and might be able to help her grow her magazine. The fact is, I did have a lot of downtime at that point, having disbanded my Women's Wisdom Circle. I wasn't sure exactly how I'd fit into Susan's publication but was open to the idea that perhaps I was supposed to be of service to her—to help support her in building her magazine.

If I'm certain of one thing as a Virgo, it's my organizational skills. I know I can always bring them to the table. I was not involved in astrology at the time, and it is not a strong suit for me anyway, but I do believe there is some merit to it, at least in a general sense. I'd now locked onto someone who didn't give much consideration to organizing. Her magazine had been in existence five or six years at that point and was floundering, really never having taken off, so in multiple visits to her home office I could see that we needed to have our proverbial ducks in a row to begin to make a success of it. I've always operated with the sense that if the desk and surrounding area are clear, as well as the filing system and anything else in that domain, the mind follows, and it's a lot easier to see where things stand. She and her artist husband, who did the magazine covers, were not even breaking even, so I figured maybe we'd been led to each another so that I could put certain practices and concepts into place that would help them get ahead. As much as I knew about business, it would also be a learning process for me as well as good exposure, as I knew very little about publishing.

In addition to putting out her magazine, Susan would hold small group gatherings in her house to study *A Course in Miracles*, a spiritually transformative book channeled by Helen Schucman and cowritten with Bill Thetford from 1965 to 1972. I was fortunate to meet a lot of people in Susan's sphere as I tried to get her organized to the best of my ability. After taking a fair amount of time to assess her situation, one day I told her that I thought what she did best was interview people and then write it up. In those days, roughly 1997–1998, computer publishing was in a nascent stage, but she also laid out the magazine that way, which she did well enough with the tools available to anyone at the time.

Unfortunately she had a tough time pitching her publication to the publicists who represented the personalities, thinkers, and New Age authors she wanted in her publication, as it certainly didn't stack up against major magazines, so getting the interviews in the first place was an uphill battle for her. Perhaps paramount to that, she was not sustaining it through advertising. Her idea of soliciting advertising was for someone to buy a $25 business-card-size space in which to feature their business or services. She'd have a dentist, or maybe a hypnotherapist, and not much else. At one point she did get Whole Foods to put in a half-page ad in exchange for having it distributed in their stores. I took stock of everything and asked her if she wanted me to create a business plan and marketing/advertising strategy to cast a wider net. She readily accepted my offer, perhaps because she had no clue what I was proposing. She just wasn't a businessperson.

I really had no idea how to proceed, so in my undercover work I decided to call a bunch of magazines—large national publications—under the guise that I was considering taking out an ad in them. Naturally they sent me their media kits, some truly amazing in scope and options. They consisted of tens of glossy and four-color pages and their latest issue, cut sheets, and more. School was in session.

Because Gina was a graphic designer, she and I created an uncomplicated, inexpensive prototype of a media kit. But we made it look fabulous. We used beautiful colored pages for the ad specs, including distribution, deadlines, demographics, ad sizes and costs, and a sample contract along with a couple of copies of the magazine, all in an eye-catching purple folder—my favorite color after I became a Reiki master/teacher. Purple is the color of Saint Germain—the color of the violet flame for spiritual protection—which at the time I used everywhere—clothes, shoes, handbags—I even decorated much of my house and my in-laws' house in the regal color of purple. Gina designed a giant sticker for the outside of the media kits, transferring the logo onto it. I'd spend my own money at Office Depot for the supplies to keep making the kits. I started networking and went door-to-door, starting to get the advertisers we so desperately needed. I prevailed upon Susan to start taking credit cards to make things easier, faster, and more attractive for prospective advertisers, something she'd not done in the past. I like to think I am someone who just doesn't sit around waiting for the ice to melt. I get in there with my pick, and that's what happened here.

Three robust, well-funded (thanks to substantial advertisers) issues into the newfound success, Alan mentioned that he didn't think I should be doing all this hard work gratis. I'd certainly proven myself, if that was ever in doubt in Susan's mind.

"Look at all the time, creativity, and effort you're putting into this, and for such a long time now. Why are you doing this for free?" he asked. "You should ask her for a commission on the ads." In fact, Alan had helped put himself through Tulane University by selling ads for the school yearbook, radio station, newspaper, and other entities, eventually taking over the whole advertising department as a junior and senior. He knew what he was talking about. He was right.

I sat down with Susan, pointing to all the work—all that had been accomplished. We now had many year-long ad contracts for substantially sized ads. I ended up creating an ad contract that people could use for every issue or for one, three, or six times a year, offering discounts contingent on how often they advertised. I created spreadsheets and files to monitor everything. She oversaw the editorial content, but I was her accounts receivables department, sending out the invoices, running the credit cards, and essentially being responsible for the overhead and all the money coming in—money I'd pursued. I even reviewed her bank statements. It was a lot of grunt work and legwork, sometimes a real grind, which I took upon myself, but I was loyal and dedicated. Funds were coming in because of my business background, diligence, and increasing expertise in her world. Where she might have $1,800 worth of advertising for an issue in a month as an exception, I'd gotten it up to $5,000, and then $7,000, and then to $8,000 and $10,000. Surely a commission was not asking too much or even a lot. In under a year, I'd taken the magazine to heights she'd not attained in more than five times that. She reluctantly agreed, but every time she had to write me a check, she would just hold her breath. I almost had to pull it out of her hand. It was the worst feeling ever—incredibly awkward. She just did not know how to give or even how to be fair and honorable. It started to feel like dark money to me—like something dirty, illegal, or something she felt I didn't deserve. I'd worked so hard and had given her 150 percent of my time, experience, and ideas, and I continued to. It just felt so uncomfortable energetically.

CURTAIN DOWN; CURTAIN UP

Among my other ideas was to put the image of whomever was being interviewed on glossy paper on the cover instead of her husband's random artwork (which people commented was often dark and foreboding) so people would be enticed to pick up the publication. Editorial ideas were not my bailiwick, but my instincts told me this would make a difference in obtaining the New Age celebrities she so desired and was having a hard time getting. Her husband was not happy about it, but she was able to convince him it was a wise business move. In short, I built the magazine into a viable, solvent, even sought-after publication.

One day Alan looked at me and said he believed it was time for me to have my own magazine. I was incredulous. *My own* magazine? Sure, it had come up a couple years earlier in the Women's Wisdom Circle, and in retrospect, if nothing else, working for Susan had been a kind of apprenticeship. But my own magazine? I just wasn't sure I could do it.

"I think you've learned everything you can possibly learn from this person, haven't you?" he asked, offering the support and encouragement that truly defined him and our marriage. I conceded. "Yes," I ultimately said. "For all I've contributed, I've not been treated fairly, and I'm disappointed." She was not who I thought she was. With that, I did take the time to meditate on it. Just after dawn one morning, I went out to the beach, talking to the universe, asking if this was the right thing and the right time … if a magazine was what

I was supposed to be doing. Was it the answer to the question about a wider platform to spread love and healing that had plagued me periodically for the past few years? The answer came back in terms of a strong feeling that it was clearly the right time and place for this venture. So what should the magazine's focus be?

In the past few years I'd learned how to have compassion for myself—whatever I was going through—and certainly for others who were struggling in their own right.

I'd attained clarity: I knew who I was and how I was to use my new life, and I knew this more with each passing day, week, and month. Beginning with my therapist, Suzanne, and with Alan's support, I'd found the courage to move forward even when things didn't make sense, learning that in the end they usually did. While I'd opened myself up to however I was guided and directed—more often than not believing I was the vessel for, not the originator of, ideas—I'd also mustered up all the creativity I could. I'd done this even as a businessperson, where creativity isn't usually the first attribute that comes to mind. I'd used that creativity to help move someone into a new financial and creative realm with a whole new look for her magazine and the means to publish what she wanted. And I'd made hundreds of connections via the kind of life I'd been carving out for myself. All of these elements were important to me and should be included in one form or another in the magazine.

The name that came to me on the beach was *Living in Balance*, soon distilled down to *Balance* magazine. I may have been on something of a tightrope at that point with no net and a churning sea of unknowns beneath me, but I faced forward and took a giant leap off my perch, as Shirley MacLaine's book *Out on a Limb* would suggest. It was time to step fully into my mission—my destiny. But I didn't know how!

LIVING IN THE QUESTION

"How am I going to do this?" Not only was I asking myself this question morning, noon, and night, but I must have asked Alan every day as well. It may have been time for a magazine of my own, but I thought we may have to fund it, and it would certainly cost a lot of money. Over time I may be able to build an advertiser base, but in the meantime, who'd want to purchase the kinds of ads that would float a magazine no one's ever heard of—with no distribution or subscriber base? Sure, I had numerous contacts, as I'd been pounding the pavement for Susan's publication for over a year, but that didn't automatically mean they'd be willing to roll the dice for mine.

Additionally, while I knew business and marketing, I had absolutely no clue about anything editorial. Common sense and marketing prowess had told me to suggest to Susan that she put notable people on the cover of her publication on slick glossy paper—something that would clearly skew more readers and very possibly be the difference between a publicist agreeing to a celebrity interview or not. But aside from that, I had to live in the question about how to fill a magazine with the right content—nothing rehashed or recycled— the kind of material that would sustain it. Somehow Alan knew it would all turn out, telling me that in a short amount of time the editorial side would be the easiest part for me. He told me in no uncertain terms simply not to worry about it. "You got this," he said. He was my messenger. As I said earlier, the message and messenger can come from many people and in many forms, so you never know who or what is putting it out there for you. In this case it was clearly my husband.

Telling Susan about my independent venture was another story. I mentioned in chapter 4 that I'm a straight shooter. That's my communication style, and frankly there was no other way to tell Susan than to come right out with it. But when I did, you'd have thought I just told her I'd repossessed her car or that I'd harmed someone she loved. Sounds dramatic, but her reaction was that severe. At that moment I thought she was the antithesis of someone spiritually enlightened—the polar opposite of the magazine she produced.

She was in my office when this happened, as she was (reluctantly) starting to write me a check for the previous month's advertising sales. I had decided to tell her then—before she wrote the check, not after. Somehow it just felt more ethical. But when I did, she cussed and made me feel wrong, disingenuous, disloyal, and just plain evil for making the decision I had. She then proceeded to threaten me, declaring I'd never have my magazine distributed in Whole Foods.

When I told her I was confident that Whole Foods distribution would not be an issue, she warned me I'd better think twice about that. Was it a threat? She just stood there in an uncomfortable silence after that. I asked for my check, to which she responded that I would never get the money (that was owed to me). I knew she was greedy, but this was almost more than I'd thought she was capable of. Though this was business, we're all human. I was really, really hurt, and I was shaking. I was not used to this kind of confrontation. I didn't deserve to be treated this way just for making a decision to start my own business after completely building hers. My back was to the wall. I toughened up and told her that if she did not pay me, she'd never get any of the advertising files. No money equals no files. That was my bargaining chip. I'd built that part of the business for her so that frankly she was still in business, and for the first time since she'd started her publication years earlier, she was making money. I'd consistently spent my own money on the computer, in places like Office Depot, and on other materials that built her business. She told me files or no files, she'd leave without writing the check. It just didn't seem to bother her.

Of course, I could have pursued her legally, taking her to court over what was owed to me, as I was almost wholly responsible for making her business viable. Ironically, she taught the Course in Miracles, but she didn't walk her talk. She had no ethics or integrity and clearly some deep-seated issues around money. No matter how much I'd done to support her, she didn't care. She believed I'd betrayed her and was going to be her competition. But that wasn't my intention, which I tried to explain to her. Producing a copycat magazine was nowhere on my agenda. It was now August of 1999. I had a name; I had a purpose; I had a direction. I knew how to get advertising, though it would be slow going for a while as a start-up. I firmly knew what to do from a design and media-kit standpoint thanks to my hard work early on. I hired an assistant, Erica, and a freelance graphic designer, Dana, and off we went.

I mulled over Alan's words and basked in the faith he had in me every day, and I set out on my own path, networking like crazy. The internet was growing up, and people directed me to different websites to query and find notable self-help genre writers and authors who may be interested in contributing to *Balance* magazine. Suddenly I had a wellspring of articles by this esteemed group—most of whom were experts in their fields—more than I knew what to do with!

I learned to put out what I needed to get it back. Often a writer queries an editor or publisher with a story idea, but I often queried my stable of contributors, telling them I needed a feature from a different angle about breast cancer or the spiritual connection between what we do and the money that comes in. Maybe it was on the art of "fear busting," but whatever it was, if I needed it, it came back to me.

In time we also got hundreds of books to review, sent to us every month from our contributors or their publishers, who also got to advertise them at the end of the bylined articles. Though I was learning as I went along, just as I had with Susan's publication, I did the wise thing and hired an editor to assist me with compiling content and editing. I also hired an art director to take the magazine to the next level, working with graphics and images.

But I'd still review every article, because I wanted to present a certain underlying theme of spirituality and empowerment for women.

We had powerful, sometimes unconventional people on our covers who had something special to share about how they'd changed their lives. We featured Tony Robbins (yes, I did the controversial fire walk!), Shirley MacLaine, Julia Roberts, Gloria Estefan, Dr. Phil, Wayne Dyer, Molly Shannon, Virginia Madsen, Leeza Gibbons, model Carol Alt (who'd come out with a raw-foods cookbook), Lorraine Bracco, Paula Zahn, and many others. Our in-depth, definitely not run-of-the-mill interviews helped to establish *Balance* magazine as a viable, exciting, innovative, inspired publication for healthy and balanced living. I cannot overstate the word *empower*, because that's exactly what we did. When you finished an issue, you knew we were different.

I recall Dr. Bernie Siegel talking about spiritual medicine and the potential for healing. I particularly recall our interview with Lindsay Wagner, who'd segued from celebrated TV star to surprising human-potential expert. She certainly would have made it to our cover with bells on, but it was our swan song issue in 2009, and at the suggestion of others, including Alan, I finally appeared on the cover myself in order to say thank you for ten amazing years and to offer a heartfelt goodbye.

I was determined not to appropriate from other sources so much of what appears in magazines geared toward happiness, health, wellness, spirituality, and personal growth and development, and I believe we achieved that. We didn't just run a feature about how to improve your business; we wrote it about making the connection between uncovering the soul in your business and achieving success. We didn't just write about relationships but about making sure you, first, are the partner you seek. Our content had a spiritual component to it but didn't shout it from the rooftops. It was subtle, suggested, like an underlying current. We distinguished ourselves from hundreds of other magazines in the way we presented the different topics—all articles embedded with a twist of spirituality. It was relevant and unique at the same time, with advertisers jumping on the bandwagon. People would tell me that the magazine was amazing and how much they enjoyed reading it. It brought a big grin to my face—happy it was being received with so much love.

WE SHINE A LIGHT

I met Liz Sterling, who had a New Age metaphysical radio show called *InnerViews*. She was a highly gifted writer and had invaluable contacts in her quiver: legends like Deepak Chopra, Wayne Dyer, and Marianne Williamson. Liz was my profile cover story editor for years. I found Californian Linda Sivertsen, known today as the wildly successful "Book Mama," whose eloquent and spirited contributions helped make *Balance* magazine come alive. I hired an advertising director, an office manager, and a sales assistant. We were becoming extremely successful. Chief among our valued advertisers were Holy Cross Hospital and Broward General Hospital, Nova Southeastern University, Auto Nation, and Bacardi, to name just a few. It's not that it wasn't hard work and a struggle at times; it's just that with it all, remarkable people and resources kept falling into place. I attribute this part of my journey to being open to receive and paying attention to everything that came through me—no matter how odd it may have looked at first.

The first bimonthly issue came out in November of 1999 (it later became a quarterly magazine), sans the extraordinary staff I was eventually able to assemble. It was just me, Erica, and Dana, boot-strappers to the core, in a home office, and it was an exciting time. I felt in my bones that all the questions I'd asked in the past couple of years about what was next for me—how to broaden my healing platform—were now answered. This was it. Perhaps that's why it all kept falling into place.

The interesting part was that at first, Susan had been right. I could not get into Whole Foods and just couldn't understand why. Around the first year of *Balance* magazine, another magazine called *Natural Awakenings*, a franchised magazine with a similar format, was coming onto the scene. I found out that neither one of us could break into Whole Foods. The publisher and local distributor of *Natural Awakenings* reached out to me about this, and we decided to join forces to get to the bottom of it. We met with a Whole Foods repre-sentative, ascertaining that the individual making the decision about what publications to let or not let in was a friend of Susan's, so that was why we were not getting in. The personal vendetta might have worked for a minute, but Whole Foods is a professional entity, and when the facts came out, that kind of blacklisting just wasn't going to last. Copies of both *Balance* magazine and *Natural Awakenings* were sent around to various managers and executives for their imprimatur, and they welcomed us to their stands with chai and cookies.

SHIP BURNING IN FLORIDA

I was still involved with everything spiritual I possibly could be. I went to many conferences and workshops—all things New Age and metaphysical. I continuously had messages coming through me, meditated, worked with Reiki, and basically embraced all things New Age. I had come so far since those fateful hours in the trunk, which I almost never thought about anymore. My life was a far cry from being eaten alive by those circumstances, the way it once had been.

My focus was my magazine. It was all consuming, and I had to give it 100 percent if it was to succeed. If asked to address a business group or appear at a seminar, my speech was no longer about the kidnapping and what happened to me during and after but rather all about *Balance* magazine and empowering women. I would walk into a room and count the number of potential advertisers I believed would help me continue to empower women.

While I wouldn't dwell on it, occasionally I'd think back even further to how I'd gotten here. It seemed the universe had been lightly tapping at me up until my near-death experience. These shoulder taps included an interest in lingering in more spiritual (called "occult" in those days, now more aptly referred to as metaphysical or New Age) sections of bookstores. But early on, I'd pretty much talked myself out of paying a lot of attention to those sections ... until I couldn't ignore them anymore.

The story goes that the great Spanish conquistador and explorer Hernán Cortés wanted his men to fight the Aztecs, but they didn't want to fight. They sat aboard their ships, unconvinced and unmotivated. Bringing them ashore under the guise of partaking in a huge feast, the men awoke the next morning to find their ships ablaze in the harbor.

"Now you've got two choices," Cortés reportedly told them. "Fight here, or die."

When I was kidnapped, clearly my ship was burned. I could not get back aboard. It was either fight for my new life, or die. It took me a while to understand that, but ultimately I fought.

I like to believe the further we get from where we started, the closer we get to where we belong. I'd started in corporate America, spent time grieving the loss of just about everything I knew and learning how to function again, and came out the other side. I came to understand that each day I was getting closer to where I belonged.

FORGIVENESS—BABY STEPS

Interestingly, in the years following my divorce from Orlando and before my marriage to Mitch, long before my deep dive into a spiritual life, I'd learned my father had gotten cozy with a lot of books on spirituality and metaphysics. My father! I mentioned he'd always been a voracious reader, and somehow his insatiable curiosity had led him there. He was also attending what were then known as Silva Mind Control (now called Silva Method) meetings in Coral Gables, founded by electrician Jose Silva in 1944 initially to raise his children's IQs. As Silva's ideas about attaining an increased state of mental awareness and projection evolved, millions of followers climbed aboard, my father among them. Learning together with him gave the two of us a stronger connection, something that had been damaged and maybe something I'd thought irreparable when he'd forced me into an empty marriage, as you'll remember from chapter 3.

But each phase of my life had fueled me, something I may have first understood in my life review. Everything leads us to where we need to be. I realized that I couldn't change him and that I needed to drop how I felt I was wronged—I didn't have to forget to forgive. I certainly didn't expect an apology. The only person that changed after I made the decision to forgive him was me. I created the space in my heart and mind, deciding to no longer be a victim. I once heard someone say that you need to deeply feel to heal. I knew that to move forward, I needed to let go of my angry feelings. I needed to connect with my emotions, the anger and pain I had been holding on to for over fifteen years. I meditated and asked to be shown through his eyes—his perspective and his why. It was so very clear to me. I now understood all the reasons behind his decision. I was able to let go, release, and forgive him. Through the process of forgiving, I was finally free and was able to take back my power. Happily, in a very short time our relationship improved to a new and loving level.

While I didn't know it at the time, in retrospect it has occurred to me that inherent in my decision to accompany my father were the seeds of forgiveness. I may not have understood or even thought about it then, but as my life continued to unfold, the benefits of forgiveness became more than an idea. Up to that point, my deep rage had been like a ball and chain around my neck—I felt mentally trapped, like an animal in a cage. After Silva, I became acutely aware of the transformational power and practice of forgiveness—whether it was forgiving my father or others for what they'd done to me, or forgiving myself for my role in two unsuccessful marriages and whatever role I'd played in lots of other things that hadn't gone well. It was extremely challenging and overwhelming, to be honest. We've all been wounded in some form or another in our lifetime. Forgiveness is not easy. In fact, it can be a long and difficult process. But

I wanted a way to create well-being, to live freely and fully, and to bring positive change into my life. I took baby steps. I chose to let go and leave behind old hurts and the past that had been defining who I was for way too long so I could truly move forward. It is said that what you resist, persists. I didn't want the pain to persist inside my body, mind, and soul any longer.

Forgiveness is not about opening up to being hurt again but instead about connecting with your negative thoughts and feelings about what happened to you. Forgiveness is something I found myself practicing often, even daily, knowing that without it, living is far more of a struggle than it has to be. Requiring perfection in others, and from ourselves, relegates us to a joyless, damaged existence from which—in that mind-set—we can never escape. We can never experience anything better. To carry around tension, anger, and resentment is toxic to body, mind, and spirit. Bitterness and resentment controls your emotions, and resisting forgiveness is like pouring acid onto yourself over and over—all the while only hurting yourself. How does your lack of forgiveness feel in your body? People have heartburn, acid indigestion, migraines, other illnesses, bitterness, and anger. It's unfortunate, but I know some people who would rather die than forgive. Ask yourself how NOT forgiving is harming you—mentally, emotionally, and physically. Who is the one stuck in the pain and negative memories? Not to be flippant, but how's that been working out for you so far? Most times, it all comes back to the fact that you haven't forgiven something in your life. Did you know that forgiveness is the highest and most beautiful form of self-love? Forgiveness opens us to love ourselves and helps us reconnect with what we were born with—what's truly inside all of us: love, kindness, and compassion.

With that, no one says forgiveness is easy, and clearly it's not about forgetting or letting anyone off the hook. The expression "forgive and forget" actually creates yet another obstacle, because most of us are not programmed to forget something painful that was done to us. Forgiveness is about getting in touch with and not holding back our emotions and feelings about what we think was done to us—from our perspective and our many, many not-rose-colored lenses. Forgiveness is also not about condoning someone's bad behavior. Rather, it's about moving on, shaking loose that behavior, and tossing it aside to keep your life on a course where joy, fulfillment, and accomplishment are not subordinated to pain and anger. Sometimes—from my newly given perspective—at a higher spiritual level it's about lessons learned. Today medical science measures our time on the planet at eighty, ninety, and one-hundred-plus years. That's a long time to live in misery and pain just because we can't come to terms with what psychologists have called the residue of the past.

As Janet and Chris Attwood taught me, what we think about, we bring about. Our lives become what we think about—the thoughts, feelings, and emotions of what's been done to us that have negatively consumed and affected us for too long. By the way, forgiveness isn't about justice. As the Dalai Lama said, "Pain is inevitable. Suffering is optional." Release the suffering that has been confining and controlling you. Let go of and release the narrative that has run your life so you can move forward. Wipe the slate clean—delete the program. Consider not waiting another minute to find true inner peace—the inner peace that has been waiting and calling to you. Forgiveness is about living a fulfilled life.

I recall that in 1994 we were in Johannesburg, South Africa, at a YPO (Young President's Organization) University dinner and had the good fortune of sitting next to Bishop Desmond Tutu when

Nelson Mandela and F. W. de Klerk were transferring the apartheid government to Mandela. I'll never forget Tutu's words for all to hear: "Forgiveness is the only future."

Here is a beautifully written poem on forgiveness by Robert Muller, former assistant secretary general of the United Nations:

DECIDE TO FORGIVE[3]

For resentment is negative.
Resentment is poisonous.
Resentment diminishes
    and devours the self.

Be the first to forgive
To smile and to take the first step
And you will see happiness bloom
On the face of your human
    brother and sister.

Be always the first.
Do not wait for others to forgive

For by forgiving
You become the master of fate
The fashioner of life
    The doer of miracles

To forgive is the highest
    most beautiful form of
    love.

In return you will receive
untold peace and
happiness.

3   Robert Muller, "Decide to Forgive," poem, http://www.robertmuller.org/decide/.

When *Balance* magazine was in its gestation stage, I knew I'd found enough confidence to pull it all together and more. My message about healing and achieving balance was really getting out there in a meaningful and purposeful form. And I wanted to do more. With all the networking opportunities—all the luncheons I attended—I felt something was missing for women. It was a lot of the "same old same old," so to speak. I wanted to do something more meaningful to help women prosper, so I created the Power Networking Luncheon concept, locking up three business clubs: the Tower Club in downtown Fort Lauderdale, the Bankers Club in downtown Miami, and the Governors Club in downtown West Palm Beach. I negotiated with each club, getting a special rate to rent space for women to attend a Power Networking Luncheon—something we called PNLs. At these luncheons, women really got to know one another as opposed to just handing out a (soon-to-be-lost) business card over the last sip of iced tea.

These luncheons were not gratuitous gathering places. They had real intention: for businesswomen to form powerful, working, enduring bonds. In fact, if you did hand out a card, the rule was you had to write the name, date, and location of the event on the back so the receiver would recall exactly how she met you—and why. No more errant cards stuck in the bottom of a purse or briefcase that you'd fish out six months later, having no idea how they got there or whose the name on the card was.

You also had to wear a name tag, and everyone had to stand up at the podium with a microphone and say a few words about themselves, especially about what they might need in their business and/or personal lives, so attendees could help you if they were so inclined. As it turned out, most women were inclined, because we created a safe and nonjudgmental environment. We had a guest speaker, and luncheons were limited to eighty attendees. We'd started out with around thirty and became so effective and successful that in time we had waiting lists. Conversations were not superficial, the kind of sound bites you'd find at most business affairs. Again, women were encouraged to ask one another how they could help. Was it a tutor, babysitter, or nanny that was needed? A Realtor? An attorney? A better bank? Financial planner? Maybe a whole new position? You could do this one on one, or you could cast a wider net at the podium. It was the kind of environment where women could be honest because it felt so safe and nurturing. These women genuinely cared about one another. We had luncheons and also annual conferences, the latter attended by up to fifteen hundred women and featuring presenters such as six-time Grammy Award winner and survivor Naomi Judd and evening events such as "The Millionaire Mind," a seminar with T. Harve Ecker, number one *New York Times* best-selling author of *Secrets of the Millionaire Mind.* Janet Bray Atwood and Chris Atwood, authors of *New York Times* best seller *The Passion Test: The Effortless Path to Discovering Your Destiny*, were among our numerous keynote speakers. There were scholarships awarded to deserving business-women seeking to take their careers to the next level.

Many of these women (me among them) came from the generation where other women were seen as competition for the few and coveted positions men held. You didn't support another female; in fact, you diminished her with disparaging remarks on many fronts. But breaking through all that was paramount. Before 1972's Title IX, where girls got to play on sports teams, women never learned about support—which may include sitting out on the bench a time or two for the good of the team. With women, it was cutthroat, and helping another female get ahead was often seen as career suicide. That was how many of us in the business world had grown up, so in the early

2000s, the idea of extending ourselves to one another was uncharted territory. We were changing the paradigm, and it felt so good; the Power Networking Luncheon was a great facilitator. Not only were women motivated about helping one another succeed, they became great friends and often business partners in the process.

To mark this very significant decade of healing, manifestation, and achievement in my life, I decided to choose a mascot. Interestingly, it was the bumblebee. Technically, bumblebees have bodies that are too big and heavy vis-à-vis their small wings for them to fly. Still, they fly in the face of all of it! Somehow the bee manages to do God's work by pollinating what it needs to, lifting off to whatever it is supposed to pollinate. It is a symbol of strength and perseverance … of getting the job done despite any handicaps that are a part of itself. It was a perfect fit for me and clearly for the hundreds and eventually thousands of other women whose lives were touched by what I was able to do with what had happened to me.

Thanks to Ellen Jaffe, I also had a (pretaped) radio program on 101.5 LITE FM that aired every Sunday at six o'clock in the morning and at midnight, which I named *BEE YOU Radio*.

Liz Sterling, Maria Soldani, and I interviewed local women about their books, businesses, and passions. We also interviewed many of the magazine's cover celebrities, including Deepak Chopra and Dr. Wayne Dyer. Additionally, I had established the Work-Life Balance Institute for Women around the time I started *Balance* magazine, a 501(c)3 nonprofit organization. The institute was essentially the umbrella under which the Power Networking Luncheons and other events took place and under which *Balance* magazine was published. It made us eligible for grants and other funding methods to help us grow and expand. The primary goal was always to foster growth, health, strength, and healing, promoting the concept of women connecting with one another to lead productive, exquisite lives. It was about empowerment.

With all that was going on around me in a practical sense, I never ignored what I dreamed about and what was coming through me from Spirit.

In a way, in building a business I was back in corporate America, but I was back on different terms. And remaining open to any information that came through me was always the key.

CHAPTER 8

MANIFESTING BALANCE

The moment you accept what troubles you've
been given, the doors will open.

RUMI

hat I know more than anything is that the only thing that is constant in life is change. We resist change because we focus on what we have to give up. The idea has been around for a long time, and I'm not the first to utter it, but for most of us, adapting to change keeps us in battle mode—with ourselves. Acceptance isn't always easy, and because change happens so often, we live in a constant state of inner turmoil. But framed differently, the turmoil around a situation involving change can be avoided. Instead of focusing on what we have to give up, Suzanne would ask me to focus on what I would gain! She would remind me that my past mistakes were meant to guide and not define me. These were powerful lessons Suzanne would teach me, and I would apply them over and over and over.

After ten glorious and—I won't lie—stressful years publishing *Balance* magazine, I was on the brink of closing it all down. I had an extraordinary staff—Erica, Renay, Sarah, and Christine—though ultimately as founder, publisher, and CEO, I was responsible for the entire operation, including the overhead. Something was in the air. Advertising and other budgets all around us were tightening, which affected us. I was facing another major change—again.

I'd always had a lot of balls up in the air, deadlines from all different directions, and that big nut to crack each month. And though my COO background had shown me how to keep the tightest of reins on our spending, it was a daily financial challenge to keep it all going. Thankfully I was blessed to have had lots of wonderful local and national advertisers and sponsors who believed in our mission and assisted us financially so we could continue to empower women with our many ideas, articles, events, products, and services. But again, things were changing on a worldwide level.

From April 2004 to April 2009, we'd held our dynamic Annual Work-Life Balance Conference & Marketplace Expo. It took place at Florida's elegant Signature Grand event center, where fifteen hundred women came together to be empowered, enlightened, entertained, and inspired by our amazing keynote speakers, panel lineup, and breakout sessions. They came to network and connect, to partner and mentor with other businesswomen. The noise from the chatter of all these fabulous women talking to each other at these events was deafening but oh, so beautiful! We thanked them with a VIP *Balance* magazine goody bag filled with gifts from our sponsors, and with the help of local business Downtown Photo, their picture would be taken when they received their name tag. When they returned the tag, they'd receive a special gift from us: their eight-by-ten picture on a mock cover of *Balance* magazine to frame and put on their desk or take home! To this day, women tell me they still have their *Balance* magazine cover picture in a frame on their desks and have kept a copy of every issue.

Sadly, our last conference would be held in 2009. Many of the advertisers and sponsors that had helped keep us afloat over the years were feeling the economic pinch. Some just plain didn't have any more money for marketing and/or to give to nonprofits (we were a 501c3). Doors were closing all around. Based on the amount of money I was able to raise, both from sponsorships for the 2009 conference and what we had on advertising for the year, I knew it would not be enough to pay for salaries, overhead, magazine printing, distribution, and all other expenses. Because I'd never taken a salary in my ten years as CEO of the Work-Life Balance Institute for Women, I could not offer that to save the organization.

I needed to make another major life decision. I needed to find a lot of money, which wasn't likely. Sadly and with much regret and unhappiness, I would have to bite the bullet and close the door. Erica, Renay, Sarah, Christine, and I were devastated.

Alan was CEO of BankAtlantic at this time, and I told him of my financial dilemma. He told me the markets were drying up and that a recession—maybe a big recession—was around the corner. I knew things were different out there, but still I was in shock. The feeling went to the pit of my stomach. For the last ten years, The Work-Life Balance Institute, *Balance* magazine—these, among other things, were my life's work—the path I'd been shown when I learned to consistently pay attention to what my guides were revealing to me. Now the economy seemed to be heading toward life support; it became impossible to ignore what was happening around me.

Additionally, with the recession looming large, my husband, who had a stellar, unblemished, transparent track record as CEO of three (eventually four) public companies on the New York Stock Exchange, serving them simultaneously over the course of thirty-five years, was being accused of securities fraud. From 2007 through 2012, with the last trial finally ending in May of 2017, he and his company, BankAtlantic Bancorp, would end up being sued once by his investors and twice by the Securities and Exchange Commission (SEC). We stood to lose everything. The events were so public, playing out in the media, that we were actually shunned at times when we walked into events. Opening a bank account was impossible, as financial institutions wanted nothing to do with us. The character attacks and news headlines—many erroneously reported online and then reverberating as they were picked up by one news outlet after another after another—were a bloodbath. Guilty until proven innocent! *What country was this?* I don't think most people comprehend the enormity of being sued by the US government. As the result of one of the trials, Alan was stripped of his chairman of the board title during an officer bar for a two-year period while his attorneys appealed. I had to watch my glorious, fair, kind, decent, honorable, generous-to-a-fault husband be hanged and quartered—when he'd done absolutely nothing to deserve it.

In 2017, when it ultimately all came out in the wash and he was fully vindicated of any wrongdoing whatsoever (many of the plaintiff's lawyers were sanctioned and fined for inventing false witnesses), it was very clear that panicked investors had acted rashly and irrationally. The SEC had jumped on the bandwagon, needing someone on whom to hang one of country's largest, deepest, most crippling recessions, during which the $8 trillion housing bubble burst. The Great Recession officially lasted from December 2007 to June 2009. Its effects continued, mounting and multiplying for months and years after that. In 2008 and 2009, the labor market lost 8.4 million jobs. It was the most dramatic employment contraction of any recession since the Great Depression and the longest recession since World War II.[4] Both Alan and I faced tremendous change, separately and together, as we never thought of ourselves as being alone in any of this.

Many people would have been fraught with fear and anxiety, even paralyzed by what was going on with them and their businesses. Maybe they'd even have seen themselves as victims. Under the circumstances, no one would wonder why we may have had strong reactions to the uncompromising stress we were under. Except that we didn't. That's not how we operated. An unusually optimistic and highly disciplined man, Alan is at his best under pressure. As a former COO, I too function extremely well under pressure, both of us knowing how to compartmentalize and go about our lives. Though *Balance* magazine was among the many great loves of my life (our kids and Alan, of course, being the others!), it was unarguably a pressure cooker. Both of our feet were being held to the fire. But I'd been there before, and so had my husband. Holding high-powered jobs, we were no strangers to conflict and dilemma. We focused and made sure any frustration we may have felt about the lawsuits and trials, and my very difficult decision about what to do with *Balance* magazine and the rest of my organization, was directly channeled into doing everything we could to effect a change for the better.

---

4   Robert Rich, Federal Reserve Bank of New York. "The Great Recession." www.federal-reservehistory.org/essays/great_recession_of_200709

We needed to work hard. I had to find a new direction, and we had to maintain unwavering faith that Alan would be vindicated. There is no denying it was complicated. At times, facing twelve jurors in that courtroom was terrifying. But we knew we were on the side of truth, and that kept us going. We clung to one another—not out of fear but for love and support—knowing that *fearing* an outcome can become a self-fulfilling prophecy. This creates more stress, anxiety, and even illness. When you know you're right, you have to have faith and stay strong in that foundation.

Still, all the positive thinking and asking my guides for help wouldn't influence a judge and jury. It's not about magic. It's about faith and trust. Alan and I had to keep our faith and optimism front and center, trusting in the right outcome—for both of us.

I asked myself what I was going to create from the demise of the magazine. I trusted that closing one door would lead me to someplace unexpected. Letting go of the fear was something that had come from my intense work with Suzanne. I tried to listen, with my head and heart, to anything my guides might tell or show me. What can any of us do when things happen over which we have no control? Bad times don't last forever. Some people may say it was all falling down around me, and certainly Alan, but we never looked at it that way. We chose not to live that way.

This was another test, or a battery of them. Alan was being tested. I was being tested. Really, who isn't? It's just that sometimes the testing is more acute than other times. We needed to pass—and not only pass, but grow as much as we could in the process. Reacting would have gotten us nowhere. We focused on being proactive. It's also a fairly well-known fact that the Chinese symbol for crisis consists of two characters: one means danger; the other, opportunity. While we are certainly not perfect, we had learned to seek out the opportunity. We all have had very painful moments in life that change our entire world in a matter of minutes—if you let them, however, they can also make us stronger. And we were now experiencing one of those moments—yet again.

THE VERDICT

My decision to close down *Balance* magazine did not happen overnight. I meditated deeply and waited for guidance about what to do. Though I may have fought it from time to time, I had to trust my knowing and listen to the messages I was receiving. I released all fear. I released all tension and anger. I released all sadness. With a heavy and forgiving heart, I needed to start the process of making plans to shut down the Work-Life Balance Institute for Women, the magazine, and everything else we did. Always totally candid with my staff, I held a meeting to tell them how much money was left in the Work-Life Balance bank account and what needed to be done. There were lots of tears. The kind of work toward spiritual, emotional, personal, and professional health my team and I did together had created a bond none of us had ever known, and knowing it was over was almost too much to bear. But there was that change element coming up again. My staff and I could accept it or not. We could let it fester and succumb to it, rendering us stale and unproductive on the next rung of what life had in store for us—each of us. It wasn't a good option.

I wanted to shut down with our heads held high, standing tall, despite the financial twister that was in the air. I didn't want to slink and slither away without saying thank you and goodbye, and that needed to be reflected in the final issue.

Our final *Balance* magazine publication would be our tenth year. Lindsay Wagner (interviewed by Liz Sterling, my cherished Southeast feature editor) was scheduled for our cover. But the universe has a sense of humor and works in mysterious ways. It seemed that during that time, the obstacles in both Alan's and my life had exploded. And they were unrelenting. But between Alan's courtroom trials and the trials and tribulations in my life, we knew we were survivors many times over, just as it's in each of us to survive our own trials. What I know for sure is that everything happens for a reason and for our highest good, though we really don't know how that good is being shown to us. Many things are not always obvious—even while it's happening in front of us. Everything is a test. I was practicing nonattachment and accepting whatever was to come, allowing it to come and go in its time. And in the midst of all this, my most trusted and constant messenger, Alan, had an idea.

FIFTEEN MINUTES OF FAME

Alan and I talked about the final cover (over the past ten years, we'd never discussed who was on my cover), whereupon he immediately floated the idea of using me instead of Lindsay Wagner. I certainly didn't want to offend a star who was our designated cover story, but by the same token, it had never occurred to me to put my face there. Alan pointed out to me that like *O,* Oprah Winfrey's magazine where she is on every cover, I should at least be on our farewell cover. I laughed at the possibility but at the same time thought it was kind of a cool and intriguing idea. Alan said it would be wonderful that our grandchildren (many yet to be born) would get to see what I had accomplished. That was all I needed to hear. Without another thought, I did exactly that.

My smiling face—though I must admit I was feeling wistful and still somewhat conflicted inside—on the fall 2009 cover is something I'll never forget. After the issue came out, occasionally people would stop me in stores and on the street, not quite realizing where they'd seen my face. They'd say things like, "Hey ... you look so familiar—are you famous?" I believe we are all famous in our own lives, in our own way, and I'd smile and go on my way. To this day when my grandchildren (all twelve of them) stop by my home office and see my face on the cover of *Balance* magazine, which is propped up next to my computer, they ask me if I'm famous! It's just as Alan had predicted, but of course I say, "No—you must be talking about Grandpa." He's the one who's famous! He's *my* hero.

CHAPTER 9

MEDITATE—YOUR PERSONAL "LIGHT" SWITCH

Meditation brings wisdom; lack of mediation leaves ignorance.
Know well what leads you forward and what holds you
back and choose the path that leads to wisdom.

BUDDHA

I t is reported that some form of meditation has been around since 1,500 BC. Ancient and modern India, China, Japan, and Greece, to name just a few, all have records of practicing various forms of it. In the Jewish tradition, Kabbalistic practices include meditation, and in the counterculture 1960s, Zen meditation actually inspired an entire movement. A couple of decades after that, my therapist Suzanne encouraged me to meditate—which actually started with instructions I'd received during my near-death experience. I just hadn't paid much attention to this powerful message.

Thirty years ago, just after my kidnapping, I now know I was a fragmented and scattered soul. I was all over the place yet nowhere at all. My old life—life as I had known it—was spiritually dead. I was flailing on so many different levels. What I do know is that I could not have healed my trauma—physically, emotionally, mentally, and spiritually—without the power of meditation. I cannot say enough that the process of meditation is the single most important, mind-blowing (yes!) message I was given while on the other side. It was my most powerful mind/body medicine. On the other side, I was told to connect through meditation and receive messages from source energy: "God, Goddess, Universal Consciousness, and All That Is." I was directed to share with the world that each person's soul wants and is waiting to communicate with divine spirit. This practice would help guide and intuit my daily life, which is my message for you. It brought me serenity and helped me deal with what was chaotic and out of control in my daily life. So much comes through meditation. Meditation is about inviting "source energy" into your life that, once inside, impels you to transcend and transform. Meditation is about controlling the "little" things that run rampant on the inside. I ask you: Are you tired of being anxious, depressed, and stressed out? Would you like to increase your awareness and consciousness? Are you ready to connect with your bigger purpose? Do you want to improve your mental, emotional, physical, and spiritual health?

Who would say no to any of those questions? So, what exactly is meditation? For the last forty-plus years, there's been a growing body of research identifying the measurable effects of meditation. Herbert Benson, MD, first wrote about a simple mind/body approach to lowering blood pressure in *The Relaxation Response*. He wrote the book over forty years ago, and it became an instant best seller. He founded the Benson-Henry Institute for Mind/Body Medicine at Harvard-affiliated Massachusetts General Hospital in 1988 (the year of my kidnapping!). Meditation has become very popular and has caught on in many professional settings, in education (at all levels), and even in the military. Meditation is a lifestyle skill and in fact is a balancing and stress-reduction technique. In the practice, a deep awareness unfolds that seems to balance the two hemispheres of the brain. Meditation isn't complicated. In fact, it's really simple yet very profound. Just like Dr. Benson's, thousands of other scientific studies and data exist that have proven its power and effectiveness for a better quality of life. It's about being in the present moment and not focusing on the past or the future. It should not be daunting or anxiety provoking in itself, as there is no judgment on whether you are doing it wrong or right. Over time you will master or at least enjoy meditation, and its benefits will astound you. Like me and the message given to me, meditation will bring you out of confusion and isolation and transform your worldview to one of clarity, connection, and compassion. It will awaken your capacity for insight and wisdom, and we can all use more of that!

BIGGER THAN OURSELVES

Meditation is not a religion, as it cuts across many religions and cultures throughout the world. I cannot say often enough that it's a powerful practice. Meditation is a form of prayer, but instead of you asking for something, it's meant for you to receive. It takes you to a deep inner peace and a higher place of awareness. And it gets better! Meditation, similar to the way that fitness is an approach to training your body, is like exercising a muscle that you build. It's a process and lifelong journey for anyone willing—or maybe courageous enough—to make it a daily and consistent practice, because it leads to significant insight. Some people are afraid of this kind of change, or change in general, which I talked about in chapter 8. But you will not be disappointed. You will be blessed and inspired when you commit to doing this kind of high-level spiritual work—daily. You will find peace, calm, inner guidance, and knowing. You will feel in control with newly acquired power and presence. You will be imbued with deep knowledge and tremendous energy as a committed light worker—and, as I tell my students, you are now on your path to enlightenment.

Meditation is a practice where individuals can use many different techniques, such as being out in nature with a walking meditation, at home, or at a place of worship—in other words reflecting, focusing your mind, contemplating, being present. For some, the beach, the mountains, or a beautiful old-growth forest is where their mind goes. The practice of meditation trains your attention and focus, creating an emotionally calm and mentally clear state—if only for a minute. Meditation is about connecting with your breath, listening to the chatter in your mind, the distracting thoughts (sometimes referred to as our monkey mind), and coming back to the present moment with your breath. I recommend you set aside the same time daily to establish a routine. Choose a spot—meditate in the same seat and location each day, locking in your personal energy to that spot. I promise that even a few minutes a day will make a big difference in your physical, mental, emotional, and spiritual life. Luckily, today there are many free techniques available online or using apps or CDs. If possible, read a book on the subject or, better yet, take a class—join a group of like-minded seekers. A meditation class can help you with many different types of techniques—there's nothing like a structured program with a great teacher to help walk the path with you.

People often ask me what I use to meditate, and my answer is that I will be forever grateful to have been gifted by spirit with two channeled, guided-visualization (guided imagery) meditations in 1996 that I produced and recorded with Steven Halpern, a Grammy Award nominee and considered to be one of the founding fathers of New Age music. I meditate to *Meditations for a Peaceful Heart* and *Meditations for Healing Stress* (please see chapter 6). Children and adults alike have responded beautifully to these CDs, which contain the background healing music and the guided imagery given to me. They continue to change lives in unexpected ways. They have been incredibly powerful for me. That's how I meditate—they are healing, restful, and relaxing, and they have been my direct ways of connecting with my source energy. I am at peace and feel joy when I'm done meditating. What I have experienced through my daily meditation practice is the value of daily coming back to my body and my senses. It has expanded my heart, my awareness, and my consciousness. Meditation has given me a sense of well-being and a more balanced perspective.

We all share a deep, special bond and powerful kinship. We are all human beings looking to reconnect with our inner light—our majestic eternal souls. We are not here on earth just to be a consumer of material goods. Through mediation we become conscious and enlightened. As you meditate daily, you will begin to look beneath the surface to connect with your spiritual path and discover your true calling. As you begin to connect with your intuition, you will begin to vibrate at a different frequency and connect with everyone you encounter through your spiritual heart. I wish this for you too—give it a try for twenty-one days—it will become your new favorite habit!

SIGNS FROM THE UNIVERSE

What I know from my own experience is that life doesn't unfold the way we expect or want it to. You don't have to experience traumatic events like illness, accidents, or crimes against you to find your purpose. You don't have to live through a night at gunpoint with adrenaline pumping nonstop out of fear that this might be your last night on earth; a kidnapping with hours spent in a sweltering trunk with your seven-year-old, hearing your heart racing and pounding out of your chest; a near-death experience; or two years in desperation with PTSD, stuck in depression and darkness, in order to understand—to forgive those who have harmed you in any way and to fulfill your purpose on earth. You now have the opportunity to forgive, surrender, learn, and transform. I went through trauma and a ten-year process of mental, physical, emotional, and spiritual discovery. Some would say my body and soul went from gas to rocket fuel, from analog to digital. But not everyone has to suffer in some form to comprehend—and practice—a different way of living. Though you may not know it, you were born to do magnificent things in your life. These messages are within you and waiting for you to activate them on a soul level. It's the life you planned before you were born. I will not try to convince or persuade you on this concept but rather offer it to be helpful. I ask only that you consider its possibilities as shown to me on the other side.

What I've learned is that the perfect blueprint for living a happy life is truly simple. Once you know the secret (meditation and forgiveness), life becomes so much easier and will unfold in ways you can't even imagine. As you meditate, you will begin to connect with your soul's purpose. The secret since you were born has been for you to become a source of light and to grow spiritually.

As spiritual beings having a human experience, we want only good things in our lives, and I would hope we would want that for others too. Unfortunately, horrific things do happen. And let me just say at this juncture that there really is *no* good or bad—everything in the universe just *is*. It's neutral until we put a "charge" on what's happened. We decide if it's positive or negative—and so shall it be from that moment on. Good or bad, know that everything happens for a reason and that it's all part of a master plan to show us (what may not be readily apparent at the time or even later) lessons we asked to be shown on a spiritual level.

The Law of Attraction says that if you don't like something, just take away its only power—your attention! You may have limited control over our out-of-control, chaotic, twenty-four-seven external world, but we have total control of our internal world. With faith, discipline, and hope, we have the power to become a formidable and significant agent of change. Healing and transformation are a process, fueled not so much by what happens to us but by our response and reaction to what happens. Reaction consists of the conditions and circumstances controlling us. Often responding in such a way to maintain peace within ourselves takes lots and lots of practice, perseverance, amazing strength, and intention. The idea of being proactive (recognizing that you are responsible) as opposed to being reactive has been around for millennia, but how many of us really think about it? Furthermore, how many of us apply it?

As you make time for quiet contemplation, below are a few questions to ponder. You might want to consider answering them in a journal to review often. I would like for you to deeply ponder and ask yourself the following:

- Are you ready to stop being a victim and forgive?

- What is stopping you from taking baby steps?

- Do you want to be happy and successful and live a life of purpose?

- Do you feel lost or disconnected from yourself?

- Do you yearn to be congruent in all aspects of your life?

- Do you know what you are on earth to do?

- Have you found your soul's purpose?

- What inspires you?

- What are you passionate about?

- What are you good at?

- Are there changes you need to make in your life?

- Are you ready to take action to follow a new way—now?

- What's stopping you from taking time to meditate—daily?

- Are you ready to share the journey with others?

As you sit, commune, contemplate, and meditate to the above questions, I know you will be truly surprised by the answers your soul will share with you. You will surely discover a deeper awareness and knowing about what the universe has in store for you to get in touch and reconnect with. The truth is simple—but are you ready to receive it now and let it unfold?

YOUR HIGHEST DIVINE POTENTIAL

Trust that you have been guided from within to read this book at this time in your life. This is your moment. As you become more open, aligned, and aware, you will deeply connect with the information I've shared. I ask you not to wait until everything is perfect and you "know" and have "read" everything to connect with who you truly are. Like me, your soul has been stirring and knocking for you to connect with your life's purpose for a very long time. You know who you are—a spiritual seeker with a quest for enlightenment. This book is just another messenger and another wake-up call. It's time to transform and integrate the person (soul) you were born to be! Stop being a lampshade. It's time to share your light with the world—on a new and luminous level. Some of us are fast-tracked, to use a corporate term, and others may never come to understand what's inside them in this lifetime—those will be the ones who will do nothing after reading this book. If I can impress upon you the idea that we are all spiritual beings in human bodies having a human experience, which can serve to put each experience in perspective, then I have accomplished one of my own great missions: to have others create a spiritual practice by meditating.

As you undertake your daily meditation and forgiveness practice, you will know on many levels—as it will be revealed to you—how exceptional you truly are—a spiritual being having a human experience filled with love and light.

THE UNTHINKABLE

Well, everyone can master grief, 'cept he that has it.

WILLIAM SHAKESPEARE

S adly, I've lost many family members in my life—my father, aunts, uncles, grandparents, in-laws, and friends of all ages. I've heard it said that the worst thing that can happen in life is to have to bury a child. I can tell you it is so. The heartache is physically and emotionally overwhelming. Our family experienced the unthinkable. Can one ever recover from this unnatural, out-of-sequence, life-changing, and heart-shattering kind of loss? Heart-shattering feels like I've dropped my most valuable and precious Limoges dinner plate. It falls to the floor, smashing and splintering into a million pieces. You can try to glue it back together, or if that fails you can even turn it into a mosaic tabletop, but it will never be what it was. Like me, it will never be whole again.

I know you don't ever get over it—you just get through it differently each and every day. Suddenly and unexpectedly losing my beautiful daughter Lauren to lymphoma on September 17, 2018, at the age of thirty-six is an indescribable pain. My body and soul ache for her. I just want her in my arms again—to tell her how much I love her. I want to run my fingers through her beautiful long curly hair. I want to hear her voice. I want to hear her laugh. To protect her from what's to come. To tell her everything is going to be all right.

I know I'll never "get over," as people persist in telling me, her passing. People ask me, "How are you?" I lie—"I'm fine." With everything I've been through in my life, losing Lauren has been the worst pain I've ever felt, and there are days when I have to wonder how the pain doesn't kill me. There is a hole that can never again be filled. I sometimes spend many days in total solitude. Days seem out of sequence. At times the thought of going along like this to the end of my own life seems overwhelming. I must admit I have questioned how I will do it—how I can continue to endure and survive this numbness and acute grief. I'm a robot—on autopilot most days. How will my heart and soul ever feel and live with joy again? I've become an empty shell of myself—tired and depressed, stumbling in the dark. I ask God daily to give me strength and guidance as I grieve and try to figure out how to grow old without her essence, her smile, her sense of humor—I ask for a path toward healing my heart and soul. I have faith an answer will soon come.

When someone passes, I've sometimes found that people tend to enshrine them. That is not my intention with Lauren, but at the same time, her extreme kindness, generosity, and many passions and accomplishments—the special daughter, sister, granddaughter, aunt, niece, friend, and fiancée she was—made her a most loving and impressive human being. The thing is, because of her deep sense of humility, Lauren wasn't the least bit interested in impressing anyone. It was never her goal. She was simply comfortable in her own skin, as the saying goes.

She and I shared so much as mother and daughter. I could write an entire book about Lauren, but suffice it to say that I'll just share with you here a very small portion of her life.

From her early years, she and I would sit outside on the patio and watch the full moon. We would sometimes see Venus next to the moon and recite *Star light, star bright, first star I see tonight; I wish I may, I wish I might, have the wish I wish tonight.* It was precious having her on my lap and enjoying our little ritual. She would close her eyes and make a wish. We would enjoy watching the full moon together throughout her entire life. She would call me from wherever she was to say, "Go to your balcony to see the full moon—quick!"

When she was about twelve, we lived in Weston—the Fort Lauderdale community farthest west. It is literally next to the Everglades. Now, besides watching the moon, we began watching beautiful orange sunsets. As she got older, she would take hundreds of pictures of these amazing sunsets. During the summer she would take beautiful sunset photos when we visited Marco Island over the Fourth of July holiday weekend. We would sit on the hotel balcony and watch the sun slowly dip down, disappearing into the Gulf of Mexico. It would take our breath away.

The fact is, Lauren was smart beyond her years—she was my moral compass. She was unafraid to offer her counsel if she thought I was about to do something that was out of character or would not serve me or others in the way I thought it would.

"You'll regret this decision; it isn't the right thing for you," she'd say candidly—which is how we were with one another: complicated on many levels but always up front and honest. Having gone through so much together, she and I shared the same kind of vision.

I can never stop loving LP, as we called her. I go to bed loving her and wake up loving her even more, if that's possible. But it is not only because she is gone and I am deeply grieving. I felt that way when she was here—each day I got to love her and our other children more than I did the day before. We would always end our calls with "I love you." The difference is that now I can no longer tell her.

LP was our youngest—an avowed vegetarian before it was fashionable and a steadfast supporter of animal rights and environmental causes. She was just seven years old when I married Alan, and she survived the kidnapping and all the hours in the sweltering trunk with me. Because of the way I was able to deal with the situation, wrapping Lauren in my arms and making it into a game we were supposedly playing together, LP never showed any signs of delayed stress or any psychological scars whatsoever. She went on, graduating college, traveling the world, and living her life with joy and a sense of freedom. She went about things with an infectious abandon. She lived for and in the moment, rushing headlong into every experience as if it were her last day on earth. Did I mention that Lauren walked at the age of eight months? She just jumped out of her baby walker and took off! I can't help wondering if she somehow knew deep in her soul that her life would be cut so short.

There was definitely a dichotomy in Lauren's personality: she was as responsible as she was free spirited (the latter is often associated with a lack of maturity and accountability—but not with Lauren). She always took care of business and certainly people. She had a knack for stock picks and business. She would call Alan and tell him, "Buy this, this, or that stock. I know they will be a good buy." And without a doubt, they were!

Our housekeeper, Petrona, was a pivotal part of Lauren's upbringing from the time she was a few months old and I went back to work until Lauren was twenty-five. She played a key role in our family during and after the kidnapping, spending that terrifying night with us on the floor upstairs and being tied to the shower in the downstairs bathroom when Alan was taken to the bank and Lauren and I were forced into the trunk. After Petrona's retirement at age eighty-eight, Lauren took care of her for five years. She found her an apartment, bought her food, took her to doctors' visits, and handled her money until her beloved Petrona's passing. There is no doubt in my heart that they are together again.

My daughter was an adventurer not only in the realm of traveling the world—which she did solo, with friends, and eventually with her beloved fiancé, Travis—but also in her appreciation of restaurants, shows, festivals, concerts, and sporting events like Miami Heat and Dolphin games. She was the most "out there" of all our five kids, yet she had a strong sense of right and wrong. She also cherished family and friends above everything. If you were her friend, you knew you were her friend. LP would do anything for you, and the same was true with family. She was the one who remembered every single birthday and every special event. She may have been immersed in her job or in some environmental or animal welfare pursuit or was somewhere out in the world doing her thing, but she never missed a birthday or anniversary or forgot about any other important event—even if we did.

It bears saying again that I never stopped learning about humility from LP. It was one of the many things that defined her. She taught me more about that all the time—and certainly about how to live a full life. Lauren chose to let only the family and a few close friends know about her illness. She determined on her own that it was best that she was not a topic of discussion whenever we would be with our friends. This was how Lauren lived her life—humble and filled with concern for others.

As much as I thought I knew and had accomplished in my life, LP found a way to show me how much more there was out there to explore. We had an extraordinary relationship, and in fact all of her relationships—many cultivated as an adult and some even retained from elementary school days—transcended differences. She just didn't see them, choosing to focus on what united people rather than what divided them.

WHEN SHE CAME

Lauren was my miracle baby, born at a time when, because of health reasons, I had been told I would have no more children. I always believed I survived being in the trunk of the car because of Lauren, knowing that rather than succumb to a terrible fate, I had to focus all my thoughts and energy on saving this amazing child's life. And it likely saved and changed mine forever!

As a child, teenager, and certainly as an adult, for LP it was brakes off and high beams on. Her passion for music began early. I had music on in the house most of the time. When I drove her to school, or anywhere else for that matter, I would always have the radio on full blast. She knew the words to most every song from the 1960s, 1970s, and 1980s: the Beatles, Elton John, the Grateful Dead, Madonna, Prince, the Police, Michael Jackson, Duran Duran, Lionel Ritchie, and even Barbra Streisand—to name just a few artists she adored. We would sing songs as they came on the radio as loud as we could with the sunroof open for all to hear. She was a sponge. When a song would come on the radio, she would challenge Alan to see if he knew the artist. It was always hilarious, because Alan had no ear for music, and Lauren would taunt him with questions. It was always fun taking a drive with Alan and Lauren. Later she channeled her mad love of music into a career in music public relations and managing various bands and musicians. Wearing her entrepreneur's hat, she founded South Florida Music Obsessed, which produced a website to shine a bigger light on the music scene, providing information that included a blog, reviews, and event listings for the contemporary regional music scene. She became PR director of III Points, bringing its annual music and art festival to life.

Lauren was always vitally interested in what I was doing with regard to my own business, though she stopped short of wanting to do the same thing. Wouldn't you know it, when she started her own company, she named it after a Grateful Dead song—"Stella Blue." As a child she would Reiki (put her hands to heal) her friends after watching me do hundreds of Reiki sessions on others. Even though most people saw her as having more of a hippie style, we both enjoyed the love of expensive shoes, handbags, and jewelry. I even had to put a lock on my closet (our family joke—she wasn't happy about it) because stuff just seemed to disappear and she took no credit for it! We went shopping and to the salon together. Manicures and pedicures gave us precious mother-daughter time. She came to all my *Balance* magazine conferences and was right up front, cheering me on when I received the multitude of community and business awards. I wanted to make her proud that I was her mother. We had a powerful and special bond and were always there for one another.

When she was thirty-two, Lauren met Travis, her soul mate. She loved him the way soul mates do. They had a wonderful relationship.

After a few years they got engaged and moved in together, acquiring two canine companions: Jaco and Fela—two beautiful Australian shepherds she loved passionately. She posted pictures of them on a regular basis on Instagram. They were what she called her boys— her "puppers." She took them everywhere. I created an album of all the photos she had sent me of "her puppers," which she proudly displayed on her coffee table.

Following her diagnosis and throughout two years of exhausting back and leg pain and multiple types of treatments and procedures, Lauren never complained and in fact was a beacon of optimism. She held us up. Travis loved and cared for her in so many ways, never letting go—both of them deciding not to let her illness deter them from preparing for their January 19, 2019, wedding. The wedding is what kept her optimistic and gave her something to look forward to—a goal that she deeply wanted to get to. Around one of her last chemotherapy appointments, she scheduled a fitting of her wedding dress—a beautiful strapless, sequined gown she purchased while in Chicago. On a sunny Wednesday morning, with a chemo port in her chest, a turban on her bald head, and in dire pain, she met a few of us at the bridal shop in Coral Gables for her fitting. Unfortunately, the inner garment of the dress was not included when it was shipped, and she was unable to have the dress fitted that day. She was heartbroken, but in her typical "can do" fashion, she took her cell phone, called the company in Chicago, and had them fix the problem. In a very short time they would FedEx her undergarment to her. We all went to breakfast together, and she went off to the hospital for another treatment. She didn't have too many days where she had the energy to go running around. The Coral Gables bridal shop had hung the dress in a very long garment bag. Lauren said, "Mom, would you mind taking the dress to your house? I don't really have a place in my closet high enough to hang it." To this day her wedding dress hangs in my closet, absent my luminous daughter, who will never get to wear it.

While I miss her terribly and have no idea how I will ever fill the space she occupied in my heart and in my life, I must say that somehow I am very much at peace with her passing. I don't have a single element of guilt or "what if" or "I could have" or "we should have." I am sure that comes from the way she and I navigated together in the world and from what I have come to know as the "otherworldly" part of my own life.

I've been fortunate enough to receive many messages from Lauren. The first was the night after she passed and there was a full moon in the sky—the harvest moon. It was one of the brightest moons I've ever seen. While taking pictures and videos of the moon from my back patio, Lauren appeared in the moon. Yes, you read that correctly—her face was on the moon! The moon was glowing like I'd never seen it before. I videoed it and sent it to the family and her friends. They all saw her shining face as well. It was a wonderful gift and brought us all to tears. Lauren has appeared to me in many dreams since and in so many other ways. I know she's sitting right next to me as I type these words.

This year of "firsts" has been incredibly difficult. Birthdays, holidays, and just about every song I hear are all triggers. I have many relapses, not just during those moments but daily. I try to do what I can to deflect and remove the intensity of my pain. I try not to get caught up in self-pity. Life, as I know so well, is too short. Even though I live every day in disbelief, I'm trying to give meaning to what I know I can't change. Her wedding dress is something I will donate to charity at some point, because I know she would want that.

I've lost a piece of myself. The death of a child is like no other loss. The stress I've experienced is unimaginable—my daughter is gone. I cry not for the amazing life she had but for her hopes, dreams, and the future she will never have the opportunity to enjoy. Her adulthood has been taken from her and all of us. But I've learned that I'm much stronger than I ever imagined, even though my life has been severely altered.

Our beloved Lauren was my courageous and strong baby girl. She had a short but extraordinary life. During the celebration of life we had for her (she'd not have wanted it any other way), more than four hundred people were in attendance—standing room only. I will forever be grateful for the love and support that was shown to me and my family during this challenging time. There wasn't a dry eye during everyone's gut-wrenching, beautiful eulogies. Her nieces and nephews (our twelve grandchildren) got up and sang the song "Season of Love" from the play *Rent*.

> *Five hundred twenty-five thousand six hundred minutes*
> *Five hundred twenty-five thousand moments so dear*
> *Five hundred twenty-five thousand six hundred minutes*
> *How do you measure, measure a year?*
> *In daylight, in sunsets:*
> *In midnights; in cups of coffee*
> *In inches; in miles*
> *In laughter; in strife*
> *In five hundred twenty-five thousand six hundred minutes*
> *How do you measure a year in the life?*
> *How about love?*

Lauren was love.

Everything happening around me up to that point was in slow motion. I was also detached and emotionless. I was in shock and not in touch with reality throughout the week after she passed. We were in a frenzy, working out the funeral arrangements, clothing, casket, who would speak, and putting together a beautiful book of remembrance. We all worked on the obituary and getting pictures to a central location for a slideshow. I had a few pictures printed and laminated to give away for everyone to remember her beautiful face. Travis and his friend Trace were busy writing a song in her memory: "My Sweetest LP." It all came together with such ease. The lyrics, the music, and the singer. I'm certain LP was orchestrating it all from the other side. I am certain she knew how much we all loved her and wanted this celebration of life to be extraordinary—as she was.

She was love. She was *my* love. Her light will never be extinguished. It shines brightly in me and in everyone who ever knew her.

From the depths of my despair, I don't know how long my grief will last. It is totally unknown and okay. But I have faith—in fact, I know—that I will recover in one form or another. With time, I will again regain my energy and gusto for life. As a pastoral counselor, I've given advice to many who have been grieving, but there's no doubt that giving advice is easier than living it. I will get through this with the love of my husband, my kids, my family, my friends, and now also by going to a grief counselor. We should not grieve alone. It's important that we have a therapist—someone to witness this time in our lives—to help us deal with isolation and unresolved emotions, as I had done so many years ago with Suzanne.

It takes a village to help us find our way.

It helps me to know that Lauren is with her grandparents and Petrona, smiling down on us. She's no longer in pain, surrounded by angels.

They Say There Is a Reason

They say there is a reason.
They say that time will heal.
But neither time nor reason, will change the way I feel.
For no one knows the heartache that lies behind our smiles.
No one knows how many times, we have broken down and cried.
We want to tell you something, so there won't be any doubt.
You're so wonderful to think of, but so hard to live without.

Melissa L. Eshleman,
Always Within: Grieving the Loss of Your Infant

Rest in peace, sweetest LP
October 18, 1981–September 17, 2018

LAUREN'S WORDS TO LIVE BY

As you have probably already determined, Lauren—LP—was an old soul and a very special young woman during her short time on earth. Below are ten simple pearls of wisdom that I hope will inspire and motivate you. It's certainly a very small collection of what she shared with friends and family—words that she lived by—truly her mother's daughter. Her good friend Tracy Block was kind enough to compile these for us, and she named them "LPisms."

1. Stop sweating the small stuff.

2. Adventure far and wide and often.

3. Create a strong inner circle of trust.

4. Perform selfless acts without bragging about them.

5. Love wholeheartedly; there's simply no other way.

6. Be there, even if you can't be physically present.

7. Stay ever so strong, even when life brings you to your knees.

8. Let go of grudges, because life is short and sweet, for certain.

9. Don't ever be afraid to say "I love you."

10. Change yourself to change the world.

LP with Tracy Block.

PHOTO GALLERY

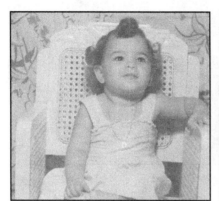

Daddy's little girl

Christmas Day with my twin
sisters, Yolanda and Mirella

Sitting on stoop with my sisters

Marrying Orlando

Me and Dad

Dad and Mom

Gina, Mom, Lauren and Dad

Gina and Dad

Me and Lauren at Oprah
event at AAA Arena

Me and Gina at holiday bash

Susie and Alan are diehard Heat Fans

Susie and Alan

Our new Blue Merle Mini-Poodle
Emotional Support Dog. His name is Blu

Susie Levan in front of *Balance* Magazine cover wall

Gloria Estefan on *Balance* cover
and her personal autograph

Bee You Radio on 101.5 LiteFM
with radio hosts Maria Soldani, Liz
Sterling, Susie Levan and Ellen Jaffe

Power Networking Luncheon at Tower Club

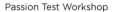

Passion Test Workshop

Conference Flyer

Keynote Speaker Janet Bray Attwood, Scholarship winners and our Bumblebee Mascot

Conference Attendees, Patricia
Sadar and Marta Sastre

Final issue of *Balance*
Magazine—Susie Levan Unplugs

Nanny Petrona with Lauren

Halloween with cousins

Lauren and Travis very much in love

Lauren and Travis enjoying
a beautiful day

Travis put a ring on it!

ACK and LP in love forever heart

Their puppers together—
Jaco and Fela

Wedding decoration—neon sign

Lauren at Beach Party

Lauren and Alan

Alan, Susie, Lauren and Travis
at the Highline in NYC

Travis, Abuela Sonia and Lauren
at their engagement party

Alan, Lauren and Susie on top of mountain in Deer Valley, Utah

Lauren resting after a long
day at the hospital

LP –even at hospital always—
had a sense of humor

Lauren was L.O.V.E.

IN APPRECIATION

Forgiveness.

Gratitude.

Love.

Getting to Forgiveness: What a Near-Death Experience Can Teach Us about Loss, Resilience, and Love—the book you hold in your hands—is the result of the steadfast and ferocious love, wisdom, and support of my husband, Alan. Thank you for being my messenger and muse and for always believing in me and never leaving my side—no matter what! Thank you for always showing me through your words, actions, and deeds how to practice being the best version of myself. I'm a better person because of you. You are the greatest joy in my life. I am so grateful that we have walked and have persevered in this lifetime together. Thank you for helping me get through all that I needed to let go of, forgive, and finally heal. Words can't describe how much I love you with all my heart and soul.

Thank you to our remarkable, extraordinary, and divine miracle daughter Lauren, the baby of our family whom I loved more than my own life, who crossed over to the other side in the prime of her life. When she passed suddenly and unexpectedly after a cancer procedure, I was thrown into an abyss—an avalanche—with no time to prepare. I sob for her life being cut so short. I am numb, stunned, my heart forever shattered into a million little pieces. What I know is that no one is ever ready to say goodbye—no matter how old they are. I know everyone we love will eventually pass away, but parents are supposed to die first!

Days and nights are excruciatingly long without her. I'm still in disbelief that she's gone. I pick up the phone to call or text her—I just want to hear her voice. I want to tell her about the full moon I want her to see. I want to see new pictures of her trips and her beautiful puppers. I thought I had gone through it all up to this point in my life, but in all honesty, grieving has been one of the most painful processes, unlike anything I have ever known. I spend most of my days in disbelief and confusion, searching for some sort of clarity. When I finally close my eyes, exhausted and ready for sleep to finally come, I ask that Lauren connect with me in my dreams. I am blessed that she shows up in my dreams smiling, happy, and healthy. I wake up crying—I miss her so very much.

My life is forever different. It can never be the same. I cannot go back. But I trust and know that God will help put me back together and that there will be light again—a life filled with hope, meaning, and equanimity. Lauren would want that for me. I know our love will continue and transcends earthly dimensions. What I also know is that God doesn't give us what we can handle: God helps us handle what we are given. Lauren, may your beautiful soul rest in peace— my sweetest LP. I love you.

Thank you to Travis for being by Lauren's side for the last five years, through her very difficult health journey. You were the love of her life. Know that it was no accident you both found each other at this precious and perfect time to share so much love and so many life-changing and challenging experiences together. Thank you for being such a glorious and outstanding man and for loving Lauren unconditionally. Words cannot express my appreciation for your patience, your sacrifices, and all the things you did for Lauren that no one else got to see. As her caregiver, I know how exhausted and drained you must have been emotionally and physically, watching her deteriorate before your eyes. It didn't go unnoticed that you handled everything with such love and patience. You were a blaze of light during this darkness for us all. I love you.

Thank you to our children and their husbands and wives for their unwavering support and kindness. I adore each and every one of you.

Thank you to our grandchildren—all twelve of them. Thank you for the privilege of being your grandma Sus. What I know is that grandchildren are pure love from the day they are born. Each of you has been such a joy and has brought so much happiness and laughter into my life. Each of you has enriched my life in ways I can't even begin to describe. Now, in the last third of my life, I leave you with a little grandmotherly advice (in no particular order, much of which you've heard me say way too many times): Be kind; be compassionate; be grateful; be forgiving; be honest. Smile, and smile with your eyes. Give a firm handshake, and look people in the eye when speaking to them. Limit your time on computers and cell phones—I urge you to unplug as often as you can. Spend time in nature and with animals. Find your passion, and have the courage to live the life of your dreams. Meditate—daily. And remember to love deeply, laugh loudly, and have fun often. You have the opportunity in your generation to be a change agent. As Gandhi said, "Be the change you want to see in the world." I am thrilled that you finally get to read "the story" of my life. I love all of you with all my heart and soul.

I am forever grateful to my many amazing, beautiful, and caring friends for your nonstop love and support—my YPO Forum sisters, my Wisdom Circle sisters, and Lauren's friends (you know who you are) who have been by my side for every step of this indescribable journey. I love you all dearly.

I would like to express my deep and sincere gratitude to Beth Herman. She is one of the most talented, compassionate, magnificent, and patient human beings I have ever worked with. I am thankful for your guidance, input, advice, support, and partnership throughout the evolution of this book. Without you, this book would not have been possible, let alone finished. Your time, commitment, energy, sensitivity, and beyond-considerable writing talents pushed and inspired me through my most trying time and darkest hours. I thank you from the bottom of my heart for your vision, talent, and perseverance. The creation of this book has been a true adventure and partnership. Thank you for taking this very personal journey with me.

And last but not least by any means, thank you to all my guides, angels, celestial helpers, masters, and others in spirit who have crossed over—who lit my path. Thank you for always and in all ways sharing your wisdom and love in unexpected ways. Thank you for inspiring me daily to live a luminous life filled with clarity and authenticity and with passion and purpose. I know I'm never alone. I am blessed for your unwavering constant guidance and protection directing me toward a path of healing and alignment with my higher self to this precious and sacred life.

RECOMMENDED READING

I'm a voracious reader. I've read thousands of books over the last thirty years—mostly in the self-help, metaphysical, and New Age genres. I wish I could list them all here for you to read, but below is a partial list of titles that I've found to be particularly thought provoking:

Many Lives, Many Masters, by Brian Weiss, MD
Proof of Heaven: A Neurosurgeon's Journey into the Afterlife, by Eben Alexander
Saved by the Light, by Dannion Brinkley
Life After Life, by Raymond Moody
The Four Agreements, by don Miguel Ruiz
Conversations with God, by Neale Donald Walsh
Heal Your Body, by Louise Hay
The Power of Intention, by Wayne Dyer
The Greatest Secret of All, by Marc Allen
The Celestine Prophecy, by James Redfield
The Power of Emotions, by Esther and Jerry Hicks

The Seat of the Soul, by Gary Zukov

Power vs. Force, by David R. Hawkins, MD, PhD

Frequency: The Power of Personal Vibration, by Penney Peirce

The Untethered Soul, by Michael A. Singer

The Passion Test, by Chris and Janet Attwood

Your Soul's Plan, by Robert Schwartz

The Biology of Belief, by Bruce H. Lipton

Minding the Body, Mending the Body, by Joan Borysenko

Long Walk to Freedom, by Nelson Mandela

Man's Search for Meaning, by Viktor E. Frankl

The Power of Now, by Eckhart Tolle

The Alchemist, by Paulo Coelho

ABOUT THE AUTHOR

Susie Levan is a spiritual warrior, entrepreneur, Life Coach, motivational speaker, certified nondenominational pastoral counselor, hypnotherapist, teacher of meditation, and Reiki master/teacher. For over twenty years, she has conducted a biweekly Women's Wisdom Circle where Susie, as a master teacher, teaches how to meditate, expand one's consciousness, find inner peace, and practice self-realization in a safe and sacred space. She lectures and conducts workshops on personal growth, self-help, and metaphysical topics.

She channeled two meditations with Grammy nominee and New Age musician Steven Halpern. She was the founder and publisher of *Balance* magazine from 1999 to 2009—a magazine directed to women for personal growth and self-development—where the focus was on health, wealth, and happiness. She was shaken to the core to awaken after her near-death experience, and from that moment on, her life's work for the last thirty years has been to empower women by having them look deep into their soul for their spiritual awakening. She lives with her husband and new mini poodle puppy—his name is Blu.

By partnering with nonprofits, all net proceeds from every book purchased will be donated to multiple charities serving South Florida.

As an author and expert, Susie is available for TV, radio, and podcast interviews in addition to lectures, workshops, seminars, and motivational and inspirational keynote speaking engagements on universal teachings and from her own life experiences for your group, nonprofit, or company.

Check out her website at http://gettingtoforgiveness.com.